by *Jeff Brauer* &
Veronica Wiles

Illustrations by
Kevin Wright

ON YOUR OWN PUBLICATIONS

Out and About in Washington DC
Copyright ©1998 by On Your Own Publications, Ltd.

Published by
On Your Own Publications
415 NW 21st Avenue, #501
Portland, Oregon 97209
Telephone/fax: 503.279.6400
e-mail: OYOBOOKS@AOL.COM

Designed and produced by
Corinna Wilborn, Grapheon Design+Type

Printed by
Singapore National Printers, Singapore

Distribution and ordering information
National Book Network
1.800.462.6420

Thank you
From Jeff: Employees at DC area bookstores provided back-
ground marketing information that made this idea possible.
They are Carlos Toledo at Barnes & Nobles; Rebecca, Mary
von Briesen and Gwen Rowe at Borders Pentagon City; Tom
Hele, Jesse Carliner and Robert Lambert Border's at White
Flint. Others who were instrumental include: Corinna Wilborn
of Grapheon in Portland, Oregon for a superb layout; Mike
Powell of Powell's Bookstore in Portland for overall encour-
agement; Heather Edwards and Doug Michel at Powell's Travel
Store; Britta Gordon at Looking Glass Bookstore; Stephen,
Jacklyn and Sarah Lim from SNP Printers in Singapore for the
best printing job available; Jed Lyons, Miriam Bass, Spencer
Gale, Michael Sullivan, Daphne Christie, Tracy Bauer, Martha
Mercier and the rest of the crew at NBN, our distributors who
place our books everywhere; Linda, Bob and Leslie Brauer for
background support. *From Veronica:* Thanks to Matilde,
Stephen, Steve and Ben Wiles for their unconditional support;
John Truong, Michael Kim, Maribel Alvarado, Maya and Aztec
for editorial support.

ISBN: 0-9643789-22

Brauer, Jeff
Wiles, Veronica
    Out and About in Washington DC
1st ed.
1. Washington DC – Description and Travel – 1997 –
   Guide books

With two years of intensive language study under his belt, **Jeff Brauer** left Taiwan for the Chinese mainland and spent the next two years exploring Asia. Along the way, he observed the crackdown on the 1989 Chinese democracy movement and quietly slipped into the Central Asian states of the former USSR soon after they became independent. With these adventures behind him, Jeff returned to law school in the US at the U of Virginia, founded OYO, co-authored *On Your Own in El Salvador* and began planning new adventures. Jeff has since graduated and spent 18 months compiling information for *Out and About in Washington, DC*.

Veronica Wiles is a recent grad of American University law school in NW Washington, DC and while clerking for a federal judge in the capital spent her free time researching this book. Veronica grew up in Bolivia where she learned new languages, met a continent of friends and had an all-around good time. Veronica has traveled from one end of South America to the other and has explored most of Eastern Europe and the Middle East, picking up even more friends along the way. She's now a young attorney and a resident-expert on fun things to do in and around Washington, DC.

Kevin Wright is an undergrad at the U of VA majoring in Architecture and Architectural History. In addition to his academic life, Kevin illustrates a daily comic strip and is a writer for the school's newspaper. His other activities include various volunteer commitments in the community and a job as manager of the varsity women's soccer team. Kevin hails from Tennessee.

Table of Contents

NEAR DC: DAY TRIPS AND OTHER THINGS TO DO WITH A DAY TO WASTE

DC: ANY DAY, ANY TIME

Washington's Best Clocks:
A tour in time

In a city possessed by both power and time, reliable, electric clocks satisfy both of these needs in the capital landscape. Through the 1950s, the government employed an official clock-winder who made the rounds among more than 800 clocks in the city. These days PEPCO, the electric company, gets paid to do the job.

Old Post Office, *Penn. Ave. & 12th St. NW, DC.* Washington D.C.'s first public clock was built for $2,600 in 1897. Its hands were so heavy that for many years the clock gained time during the first 30 minutes of every hour and lost time the last 30 minutes.

Capitol Hill, Statuary Hall, *Old House of Representatives chamber, DC.* Perhaps the most famous clock in the city, the seven-foot marble Car of History still runs on the 1837 mechanics installed by a Massachusetts-based clock maker. One-time President and Congressman John Quincy Adams wrote a sonnet to the clock and discreetly placed it inside, where it was discovered nearly 100 years later by a worker giving it a cleaning. This is one of a handful of clocks on Capitol Hill that doesn't run on electricity.

US Naval Observatory, *34th & Mass. Ave. NW, DC.* The home of the Vice President is also home to the city's most exact clocks. More than 20 atomic clocks, a hydrogen master clock and clocks to illustrate the evolution of measuring time are on display.

Italy in DC:
Lotsa pasta

Washington doesn't have a Little Italy, but it does have a lotta little bits of Italy, give or take a foreign accent or two. Washington once had an Italian section, centered around the **Holy Rosary Catholic Church** *at 3rd & F Sts. NW, 202.638.0165* (masses in English and Italian). But the white flight, racial rioting and interstate freeways spurred a move to the suburbs. It is there, mostly in Prince George's County, that the remnants of DC's Little Italy exist.

Casa Italiana, *next door to Holy Rosary, 595 3rd St. NW, DC,* Churchgoers, the local Italian speaking community and immigrants gather for coffee at Casa Italiana after mass and during the week. Italian language courses are offered inside, too.

A. Litteri Italian Groceries, *4th & Morose Sts. NE, DC, 202.544.0183.* Squeezed between other ethnic grocery marts but still the place to get real Italian cheese, sausages and produce.

The Catania Bakery, *1404 N. Capitol St. NW, DC, 202.332.5135,* serves up fresh loaves of Italian bread.

Libraries in DC:
To read and roam

The DC area is home to more than 500 libraries, including nearly 200 in the city alone. Some are eclectic, others restrict entry to members and, ahem, intellectuals. But, whatever the interest, there's a library to match suit, and there you are certain to discover new friends who love the same books and new books that will become your new friends. Here are a sampling:

Garden Library, *1500 Glenallen Ave., Wheaton, MD, 10am-5pm M-F, 12-5pm S-S, 301.949.8231.* The Garden Library is filled with books that will inspire the novice gardener and enlighten the expert horticulturist. Books are non-circulating, but the pots of plants that line the wall and the conservatory next door make the most important lessons (water regularly and plenty of sunlight) easier to remember.

Historical Society of Washington DC, *1307 New Hampshire Ave. NW, DC, 202.785.2068.* The library at the historical society, housed inside the ornate Christian Heurich Mansion, traces the city's sociological roots. The archives are packed with photos that date back to the mid 19th century.

Lloyd House, *220 Washington St., Alexandria, VA, 9am-5pm M-Sat., 703.838.4577.* The Lloyd house is Alexandria's first public library and serves now as a reference, not a checkout, library. Its stacks are filled with collections that trace the history of the Commonwealth of Virginia, the genealogy of its people and the South in general. There are special collections with information about the Civil War and about each of the counties in the State. The two reading rooms upstairs are lighted by turn of the century chandeliers.

Kennedy Center Educational Resource Center, *Kennedy Center Roof Terrace, 2700 F St. NW, DC, 10am-6pm T-F, 11am-8:30pm Sat, 202.707.6245.* The Kennedy Center library boasts a magnificent view of the Potomac River and a thorough collection of magazines and books related to the fine arts from all over the world. Once run by the Library of Congress, the Resource Center has been recently "downsized," like the rest of DC, so its collection is somewhat reduced.

Washington Calligraphers Guild Library, *Strathmore Hall Arts Center, 10701 Rockville Pike, Rockville, MD, 301.330.9234.* This very exclusive library about the ancient art of calligraphy opens one day each month for viewing the 200 or so books in the collection. The limited collection represents a sampling of the finest calligraphy from different ages and the far corners of the earth. It shares company with a single table to take notes and two very comfortable, though ancient, armchairs in which to relax. Strathmore Hall itself is home to a revolving exhibition of art, and the grounds play host to a regular series of concerts throughout the summer.

Famous DC Spying Spots:
Undercover capital

In the Bellevue Hotel on Capitol Hill, *15 E St. NW, DC, 202.638.0900, Rm. 524,* former head of Soviet military intelligence Walter Krivitsky either killed himself or was killed on February 9, 1941. Krivitsky defected from the USSR after Stalin purged and subsequently murdered the KGB brass. After Krivitsky testified to the House of Representatives Un-American Activities Committee that Stalin tracked down his foes abroad and kidnaped or killed them, some say that Stalin threatened his family members who were still in the USSR. You can read about it in Krivitsky's memoirs, *In Stalin's Secret Service.*

4100 Nebraska Avenue NW, DC, was the British double agent Kim Philby's DC haunt. Philby knew that Britain's spy service, the M15, was closing in on him and he conspired in this very location to escape to Russia with other British double agents.

4936 30th Pl. NW, DC, was former FBI director J. Edgar Hoover's home. When he wasn't in the office or knocking back a gin at the Mayflower, Hoover was at home in his brick home with (still) bulletproofed windows, rosebushes and master bedroom balcony.

2552 Belmont Rd. NW, DC, is the former Soviet Military Office, de facto headquarters for the KGB. The Soviets did their best to make the building nondescript, but the FBI eyed it from afar, day in and out.

South African spy Jennifer Miles lived at **2800 Wisconsin Ave. NW, DC.** The Cubans recruited her, the FBI tracked her and it is said that the White House, Defense Department and State Department slept with her. In any case, the FBI stopped keeping track when the number of amores topped 100. In the end, when she was confronted by the FBI, Miles confessed her Cuban ties and quietly returned to South Africa.

Watergate Building, 2600 Virginia Ave. NW, DC, was where the Democratic National Committee had set up their headquarters to defeat President Nixon. On June 17, 1972, five burglars, including an aide to the Republican's Committee to Re-elect President Nixon, were caught wearing surgical gloves and carrying bugging devices and other incriminating evidence. G. Gordon Liddy, local radio talk show host extraordinaire, was a member of the group.

The Georgetown Pharmacy, 1344 Wisconsin Ave. NW, DC, was where Elizabeth Bentley rendezvoused with Soviet secret police chief Anatoli Gromov. Bentley routinely funneled data from US bureaucrats and columnist Walter Lippmann's files to the Soviets. Later, when she testified in front of the House Un-American Activities Committee with two artificial red roses in her hair, she was dubbed the "Red Spy Queen."

At the second utility pole east of the intersection of Watts Branch Circle and Ridge Drives, MD, is where the Soviets left notification, in the form of a 7-Up can, for retired US naval officer John Walker, Jr. that they were ready to exchange cash for documents. Documents in hand, stuffed inside a grocery bag, Walker left his reply, another 7-Up can, on the bottom of a utility pole at the intersection of Quince Orchard and Dufief Mill Rds., MD.

Russia in DC:
Where to get a Russian bear hug

I f you're a fan of Borscht, or otherwise still have feelings for Gorbachev, there's enough of Russia in the capital to stay your nerves. Besides some of the obvious points of interest for Russia-watchers, like restaurants, there's a host of landmarks that were originally owned by prominent Russians and handed down over the years, albeit with a little bit of Moscow hidden in the walls.

Hillwell, *4155 Linnean Ave. NW, DC, 202.686.5807,* the very decorated, stuffed-with-antiques home of Merriweather Post has been preserved as a museum. Post's husband was a US ambassador posted to Moscow in the 30s when the fledgling Bolshevik Republic sold many state treasures in an effort to raise funds. Thereafter, Post's house became something of a center of Russian antiquities and she continued to scout for the best Russian treasures for sale for the rest of her life.

The St. John Russian Orthodox Cathedral, *4001 17th St. NW, DC, 202.726.3000,* and **St. Nicolas Orthodox Church,** *3500 Mass. Ave. NW, DC, 202. 333.5060,* have served as the center of the local Russian religious community for many years. Church social functions include typically Russian cultural activities, like folk dances and singing. As a concession to the US born children of Russian immigrants, perhaps, both churches host services in English, too.

Dumbarton Oaks, *1703 32nd St. NW, DC, 202. 339.6400,* has a post-Byzantine icon art collection with a special display of jewelry.

The Von Brahler Gallery, *304 Russel Rd., Alexandria, VA, 703.683.7474,* has an impressive display of contemporary Soviet art.

The Library of Congress' European Reading Room, *Jefferson Building, 101 Independence Ave. SE, DC, 202.707.5522,* has the country's best collection of Russian literature and magazines.

Victor Kamin Bookstore, *4956 Bolling Brook Pkwy., Rockville, MD, 301.881.5973, 9am-5pm M-Sat.,* is devoted to the collection and sale of books imported from Russia or produced in Russian. It is also apparently something of a haunt for the CIA Russian ghouls.

C&O Canal:
DC's first beltway

The 185-mile Chesapeake and Ohio Canal, completed in the mid 19th century, is a history lesson and a jogger/biker's paradise rolled into one. The C&O originates in Georgetown and is studded with ancient, intricately detailed bridges, and 74 locks. It climbs and winds slowly to Cumberland in western Maryland.

The National Park Service, *202.619.7222,* has a map of the entire length of the C&O, including details about where it can be accessed and some of what there is to see along its course. Two good ways to enjoy and learn about the C&O are to walk or bike it in segments on good weather days, and to hop in the car and drive off to explore seldom-visited locks that sit beside the quaint, old towns that dot its course.

Capital Churches:
Beautiful places to worship

DC churches are everything the rest of the city is not: quiet, relaxed and built to look good and impress the Gods. And there are all types, including Greek Orthodox, Episcopal and Roman Catholic, some with colorful mosaics, others with grand organs and all with plenty of peace and quiet! Here are a few of the more interesting ones:

Metropolitan African Methodist Episcopal Church, *1518 M St. NW, DC, 202.331.1426.* This Victorian Gothic church is squeezed next to another major landmark: the Washington Post. The Metropolitan, a stop on the underground railroad during the Civil War and earlier, is one of the city's most prominent African American churches where famous Americans, including Jesse Jackson, Frederick Douglas and others, have preached.

Washington Cathedral, *Mass. & Wisconsin Aves. NW, DC, 202.537.6200.* In addition to being the city's tallest building, the Washington Cathedral is also among its most ornate and definitely the most distinctively Gothic. Though the Cathedral is officially Episcopalian, most worshippers there are of other denominations. This is the second largest cathedral in the country (NY City's St. John the Divine is the largest) and it has a nave that is a full one-tenth of a mile long (the world's fourth largest). More than 200 stained windows filter the incoming sunlight and included on them are scenes both from antiquity, such as events out of the old and new testament, as well as modern events, like a tribute to the doomed Apollo 11 mission with a moon rock in the center! The nine surrounding chapels explore different themes, including one devoted to children with miniature chairs and a small pipe organ. Tours are offered 10am-3pm M-Sat.

Christ Episcopal Church, *118 N. Washington St., Alexandria, VA, 703.549.1450.* George Washington and Robert E. Lee worshiped here in the heart of Alexandria. Most of the original woodwork inside is original, and you can still see the pews that Washington and Lee used.

Saint Sophia Greek Orthodox Cathedral, *36th & Mass. Ave. NW, DC, 202.333.4730.* Saint Sophia has some spectacular Byzantine mosaics that cost the church more to buy than the building cost to construct.

Islamic Center, *2551 Mass. Ave. NW, DC, 202. 332.8343.* The call from the minaret announces prayer five times each day, the compound smells of sweet, eastern fragrance, and colorful, individually painted Turkish tiles line the walls of this mosque.

Franciscan Monastery, *1400 Quincy St. NE, DC, 202.526.6800.* The monastery trains missionary priests and houses about 35 friars. The church was constructed to memorialize the holiest Christian shrines, some of which are recreated here in miniature.

Shrine of the Immaculate Conception, *4th & Michigan Ave. NE, DC. 202.526.8300.* The blue-domed National Shrine with its thin tower was constructed by volunteers who represented many local ethnic groups and religions. Marble from all around the world was used to construct the building and each mantle, altar and statue represents a different sector of the community. The Shrine is the country's largest Roman Catholic church. Notice that the inside marble walls contain, among other things, the names of many of the people who helped construct it and, in case you're interested, a memorial to Yankee's slugger Babe Ruth. The big attraction, though, is the Crypt Church on the lower level with its onyx altar and the 57 chapels situated throughout the shrine, each decorated to express a particular vision of the Virgin Mary.

Cathedral of St. Matthew, *1725 Rhode Island Ave. NW, DC, 202.347.3215.* This is the church where the funeral for President Kennedy was held. There are famous mosaics of St. Anthony of Padua and much Romanesque, spacious architecture to gaze upward at.

New York Avenue Presbyterian Church, *Lincoln Church, 1313 New York Ave. NW, DC, 202.393.3700.* President Lincoln attended service here during his tenure as US president and memorabilia from that era is on display. There are also some 19th century pews and a parlor maintained in good form.

Christ Church (Washington Church), *Cameron & N. Washington Sts., Alexandria, VA, 703.549.1450.* This was the place of worship for America's founding father, George Washington. The pew Washington purchased for his exclusive use when the church opened in 1773 is on display, and if you sit on it you'll see what Washington saw during his trips to church, albeit with the benefit of electric lights. Across the aisle from Washington's pew is one rented by General Robert E. Lee, who attended church here 80 years after the first president but still a full 15 years before the Civil War. As the tour guide will note, Christ Church is in similar shape as it was when these important Americans worshiped here, and the cemetery in the churchyard has its own, mostly preserved history engraved on the tombstones.

African American Roots in DC:
Black capital heritage

DC's black heritage survives in many pockets of the city, from gravesites that date back to the early 19th century to churches that once served as places of worship for prominent African Americans. Some stops, like the homes of important black Americans, are museums to a city in a different era, albeit with their interiors intact. Others are witness to a vibrant city that has evolved demographically, like the graveyards which are situated in Georgetown, and socially, like the Mt. Zion Church which began its incarnation as an offshoot of a white church nearby and evolved into a forum for presidents and prominent African Americans.

The Female Union Band Cemetery in Georgetown, *27th & Q Sts. NW, DC, behind the nearby apartment building,* now overgrown by weeds and nestled behind an apartment house, recalls the existence of a local and prominent black community that resided here in the late 18th and early 19th centuries. Not many of the tombstones are legible, but the site helps explain the history of Georgetown's once thriving black community, which once was more than half the local population. The cemetery's history is related to the nearby Mount Zion United Methodist Church, which was founded after blacks left the Montgomery Street Church that was located next to here.

The Mt. Zion United Methodist Church, *1339 29th St. NW, DC,* was founded by black parishioners in 1826 who wanted their own church. Next door is the church's archives with records of the many thousands who have worshiped and lived nearby.

Howard University's quadrangle, *2400 6th St. NW, DC,* is a center of young African American culture and is surrounded by many buildings, including the impressive multi-spired chapel, that comprise the city's first predominantly black university.

Rock Creek Park:
Capital woods

Washington's forest has been off-limits to developers since the Civil War, when the Army Corps of Engineers proposed that part of the rapidly expanding capital remain green. It was a radical concept, especially since so much of the surrounding land was being used to house factories and other buildings. But in time the concept charmed Washingtonians who now have access to a closely situated complete getaway. Some of the big sites to visit in Rock Creek Park are these:

Fort DeRussy, *Oregon Ave. north of Military Rd. NW,* DC, is one of many forts constructed near the capital during the Civil War that helped defend against an attack by Confederate leader Jubal Early and his troops.

Pierce's Mill, *Glover Rd. & Tilden St. NW, DC, 202. 426.6908,* is the city's only remaining mill and is located in the Park. Isaac Pierce was a Pennsylvania Quaker who built his mill in the 1820s to grind grain for local farmers. The mill operates today, albeit on city supplied water, and still churns out fresh corn meal and flour.

The Rock Creek Nature Center, *5200 Glover Rd. NW, DC, entrance off Oregon Ave., 202.426.6829,* hosts talks about and walks through the Park, including the occasional one under the stars. There's also a planetarium that is opened for monthly telescope viewings.

Rock Creek Horse Center, *Military and Glover Rds. NW, next to the Nature Center, DC, 202.362.0117,* rents horses and gives riding lessons. It is also a good source of information about riding and hiking trails that lead through the Park.

DC Cemeteries:
Resting place of early capital inhabitants

A local cemetery is a city's de facto history book. Prosperity, plague and war are all indelibly and permanently carved into the grounds at a cemetery. Indeed, at a national cemetery the history of an entire country is scripted upon the headstones inside the gates. Here are some of the nicer or more noteworthy local cemeteries that are worth a *temporary* visit.

Oak Hill Cemetery, *30th & R Sts. NW, DC,* is where many of the people who founded the city were buried. It is meticulously maintained.

Congressional Cemetery, *1801 E St. SE, DC,* is a bit of cultural history book. John Phillip Sousa, the musician who wrote many of the famous melodies that we hum on July 4th, and J. Edgar Hoover, who merely tried to listen to what we were humming on the fourth, are buried there, as well as Belva Lockwood, the first woman to run for US president.

Quantico National Cemetery, *18945 Barnette Cir., Triangle, VA, first Quantico exit off I-95 south, 703.690.1996,* opened in 1985 and takes many of the funerals that were once assigned to Arlington National Cemetery.

Hollywood Cemetery, *at Cherry & Albemarle Sts. in Richmond, VA,* is a virtual history of the Civil War. Jefferson Davis, president of the South during the Civil War, is buried there as are many of the prominent soldiers who struggled for the Confederacy.

DC's Weird Tourist Sites:
Capital tourist splash path

A trip to the Air and Space Museum isn't half as fulfilling as a trip to some of what is on DC's slightly wacko tourist path—the places that nobody except the 30-year commuter would hear about, but which would make the rest of us do a double-take. Indeed, even in DC there are surprises, and some of the them are big.

Statue of General Winfield Scott, *Scott Circle at 16th St. NW, DC, 6 blocks north of the White House.* General Scott was a hero of the war with Mexico and, as his compatriots and descendants knew, he never rode anything but a stallion in battle. Nonetheless, the sculptor of the statute placed Scott on a mare, to the shock of everyone who showed up at the unveiling. What was the sculptor to do but to agree to a metallic sex-change? After sculpting an extra piece and welding it on, the correction was completed and to this day it remains there for everyone to see.

Freedom Statue, *the 19½ foot statue atop the Capitol dome, DC.* Freedom was originally sculpted as a nude, but that drew the ire of a few congressmen 150 or so years ago. When the sculptor threw a metallic robe around her, southern senators complained that she looked like a freed slave. Finally, the sculptor added a headdress of feathers, which makes Freedom look Indian and, for whatever reason, more politically palatable to the aged few who made our laws back then.

Jefferson Building, *101 Independence Ave. SE, DC, Library of Congress.* This late 19th century building, with its ornate interior, has many strange books and a particularly strange display. On the lower windows on the outside wall are mounted sculptured heads that represent the "33 major races of the world," as it occurred to the sculptor one century ago. Included among the 33 are the head of a blonde European and a brunette European, in case you look hard and can fathom the difference.

Washington Monument, miniature edition, *next to the actual Washington Monument, under a PEPCO iron plate, DC,* is a 13½ foot miniature of the real thing. If you're lucky enough to spot it (the Park Service doesn't lift the plate very often) you'll see an oddity that was constructed to help determine if the big Washington Monument was sinking into the earth or leaning. Actually, when it was first constructed the big monument did begin to tilt, although it has since been yanked back upright.

Weighing Station for the Washington Canal, *SW corner of 17th St. & Constitution Ave. NW, DC.* The city in the 19th century was a different sort of town. For one thing, there were fewer tourists. For another, there was a canal running through the city, and the Weighing Station is there to prove it. When the architect of the city, Pierre L'Enfant, drew up his plans for the city, he included a grand canal that paralleled Constitution Avenue, widened into a small lake near the Ellipse and continued past the then public market further inland before turning back towards the Potomac near the Navy Yard. In fact, the canal was built. In time, though, it died a slow death that was caused in part by the advent of the railroad which made water transport impractical. When the canal became polluted the government filled it in with dirt but kept the Weighing Station.

DC Zero Milestone, *in the ellipse next to the National Christmas Tree, NW.* It wouldn't be accurate to say that all roads lead to DC, but those that do are measured from DC's Zero Milestone, situated on the north side of the ellipse. Nearby is a small granite shaft which stands in gratitude to the original landowners of DC, who agreed to sell everything to the government for the land that would become the nation's capital.

Shenandoah's Pride, *US Highway 11 N, Mt. Crawford, VA, 540.434.7328.* Shenandoah's Pride is not the place to go to milk a cow by hand. Go figure. There are 125,000 cows at Crawford farm, and they don't have more than a handful of stools, pails or workers. The milk industry of the 1990s is a high-tech business. Computers milk cows and balance the amount of food they eat versus the amount of milk they produce. Milk jugs are manufactured faster than one per second, 24 hours a day. And, miraculously, the folks at Shenandoah's Pride have discovered the delight of other milk products, like chocolate drinks and even ice cream sandwiches, all of which are available at the end of the tour, in case you're wondering, hungry, or both!

Embassy Row:
Public diplomacy

E mbassies and international organizations are assigned huge responsibilities like representing fractious homelands or funding development. Because this group is housed in some of the city's snazziest dwellings, they are prime targets for public viewing when they open their doors to the rest of us. Fortunately, most do invite the public on occasion. Here are some contacts:

France, *4101 Reservoir Rd. NW, DC, event hotline 202.944.6400.* The French embassy has a special complex that is intended to showcase French society, and a 300 seat theater for occasional movie showings.

England, *3100 Mass. Ave. NW, DC, 703.271.0172 or 202.462.1340.* The UK occasionally hosts a series of plays by a local troupe, with shows in the embassy rotunda.

Italy, *1601 Fuller St. NW, DC, 202.328.5500.* The Italian embassy hosts art shows, including many that showcase the Renaissance.

World Bank, *G St. between 19th and 20th Sts., DC. Ask for the community affairs division, 202.477.1234.* The World Bank hosts free concerts at its auditorium.

Organization of American States, *17th & Constitution Ave. NW, DC, 202.458.3718.* The elaborate, unbelievably ornate headquarters of the OAS plays host to a representative sampling of musicians from throughout the Western hemisphere. It also has an indoor garden and showcases artwork from Latin America.

Germany, *4645 Reservoir Rd. NW, DC. Call the cultural department to be put on the mailing list, 202. 298.4000.* The German embassy has a packed schedule of concerts, mostly by groups from Germany, as well as lectures and plays that continue throughout the year.

Brazilian-American Cultural Institute, *4103 Conn. Ave. NW, DC. Call to be placed on the mailing list, 202.362.8334.* Brazil's auditorium hosts a few events each month, including films and receptions at the beginning of art exhibitions.

Canada, *1771 N St. NW, DC. Call the events hotline and ask to be placed on the mailing list, 202.682.1740.* Canadian musicians and dance troupes regularly travel to the US, and the embassy often helps promote the events.

DC's Finest Mansions:
Capital wealth on a tour

V isits to the city's finest homes is a distinctly private affair and a chance to appreciate how the local aristocracy once lived. The art inside these homes is not as extensive as that displayed in the city's museums, but the settings are more personal and there are fewer tourists nearby. Also, unlike most public buildings, each old house has its own private, and usually very interesting, history.

Anderson (Cincinnati) House, *2118 Mass. Ave. NW, DC, 1-4pm T-Sat., 202.785.2040.* This mansion was constructed in the early 1900s for a fee that would still buy a mansion: $1.5 million. Needless to say, back then it bought much more, like a very large ballroom, intricately carved ceilings and both art and sculptures by artists whose other works are on display across town in the museums. The Andersons liked to entertain, and they were perfectly situated to do that. Mr. Anderson was a career diplomat and his wife was Boston's wealthiest heiress. Their Great Stair Hall, ornate French parlor and marble floor made this mansion an important stop on the DC social circuit a few generations ago. Relics from the Revolutionary War are exhibited on first floor, while the second floor contains furnishings that date to the 1930s when the Andersons sold it.

Hillwood, *4155 Linnean Ave. NW, DC, 202.686.5807.* This is the creation of Marjorie Merriweather Post, the benefactor who contributed much money and many buildings to DC's landscape. This creation, on 25 acres of land beside Rock Creek Park, houses a museum of Russian art and nearly 30,000 other objects that Ms. Post collected when her third husband, Joseph Davies, served as the US ambassador to the Soviet Union in the 1930s. At the time, the USSR was trying to raise money by selling its treasures, and Ms. Post was a convenient customer. Two of the famous Fabergé Imperial

Easter Eggs are on display here, as well as many paintings of Russian nobility and leaders who predate the communist revolution. Reservations are recommended for tours.

Tudor Place, *1644 31st St. NW, DC, 202.965.0400. Tours 10am-3pm T-Sat.* Tudor Place was owned for nearly 180 years by the family descended from Martha Custis, granddaughter of George Washington, and her husband Thomas Peter. They commissioned the architect of the US Capitol to enlarge the residence. Through the years the descendants of Ms. Custis have lived here and experienced the city as it grew and otherwise changed. They've also been part of the city's history on occasion and many famous visitors have been guests here including Lafayette, Francis Scott Key, Henry Clay, Daniel Webster and John Calhoun.

Decatur House, *748 Jackson Pl. NW, DC, 202. 588.6210, open all days of the week.* The Decatur house has two parts, upstairs and downstairs. The first floor housed Stephen Decatur, the naval hero who is the namesake of this impressive building. Upstairs, life in Victorian-era DC survives since Edward Beale, a local businessman, purchased the house and added classical decoration from that era. Decatur lived here for less than two years, when he died from wounds incurred in a duel with another seaman, John Barron. He wife then sold the house to raise money and, fifty years later, it was purchased and restored by Beale. The architecture, furnishings and legends told by guides make it memorable.

Touring the Federal Government in DC:
Walking through the wheels of power

A merica pays the water, electricity and salaries at the fed's government buildings. And, since so many government building are congregated in DC, someone powerful made the wise decision to let the rest of us in, albeit on a tour. Wear walking shoes to handle the long halls, watch out for columns and leave anything that will set off a metal detector at home.

The Bureau of Engraving and Printing, *14th & C Sts. SW, DC, 202.622.2000,* has a self guided tour of the facility that prints our greenbacks and most everything else official. There's a display about counterfeit money and lots and lots of security guards.

The FBI, *E St. entrance between 9th & 10th Sts. NW, DC, 202.324.3447,* is shrouded in what looks like the city's largest bunker. The tour, which passes confiscated loot, drugs and other items equally dangerous or illegal, is pretty bland but has a surprise and very loud ending.

The Library of Congress, *1st & Independence SE, DC, 202.707.5458,* has America's snazziest middle age reading room, in addition to 25+ million books. The tour passes through a few of the minor reading rooms and includes a peek at the rare Gutenberg Bible.

The Pentagon, *off I-395 in Arlington, VA, 703. 695.1776,* is the world's largest building, judged by floor space, and the tour passes zero of the many high-tech goodies inside. Regardless, it is memorable to be inside a structure that is the office space of 25,000+ employees and which is, no doubt, the dead center target of some rogue nation's missile system. Be prepared to walk.

The Supreme Court, *1st & E. Capitol Sts. NE, DC, 202.479.3499,* is a tour in action when the Court is in session. At other times, tours pass through the main rooms and halls. Unlike "real" court, a tour of the Supreme Court permits talking.

Capitol Hill, *east end of the Mall NE, DC, 202. 224.3121,* is host to a series of tours, not all in the same building. The tours pass through everything that shows up on a postcard including the Rotunda, the old Senate chambers and the room where the Supreme Court was situated more than a century ago.

The White House Tour, *1600 Penn. Ave. NW, DC, 202.456.7041,* passes through many of the mansion's famous, colorful and temporarily deserted rooms. In fact, when the President is out of town, the tour is sometimes re-routed through the court yard that glances the Oval Office. Security guards occasionally double as tour guides (at least the ones who aren't carrying guns), but the experience is otherwise a walk-through-affair, including an exit via the main door—remember to take a camera along.

DC Tea:
Caffeine alternatives

There is such a thing as tea time, and it doesn't merely exist on Greenwich time. If you indulge, you'll be pleasantly surprised to discover that tea does not cause a caffeine twitch like the one you'd get if you downed a Java alternative. Tea time is usually around 3:00 to 4:30 pm at these locations. Don't forget to ask about tea sandwiches!

Four Seasons, *2800 M St. NW, DC, 202.342.0444, 3-5pm M-Sat.* The Four Seasons is a great place to hang out and everyone seems to be making deals. Tea is served with scones and scuffles, both chocolate and strawberry.

Hay-Adams, *16th & H NW, DC, 202.638.6600, 3-4:30pm M-Sun.* The Hay-Adams is so realistically ancient that you might bump into one of the country's founding fathers. Tea is served with finger sandwiches and scones in the Lafayette Room.

Henley Park Hotel, *926 Mass. Ave. NW, DC, 202. 638.5200, 4-6pm every day.* This early 20th century revival is open a full hour later than other tea rooms in the area. Tea is served with scones in the Wilkes room, a traditional New England room with a fireplace.

Strathmore Hall, *10701 Rockville Pike, Rockville, MD, 301.330.9234, 1pm T-W Sept through May.* Tea time in an ancient mansion in the middle of rush hour hubbub is what Strathmore Hall, an old mansion, is all about. Tea is served with scones, bread and fruit in the music room to live music.

Hillwood, *4155 Linnean Ave. NW, DC, 202.686.8893, 2-4pm T.-Sat.* The Hillwood in Rock Creek Park is set in the Hillwood estate and overlooks gardens and a couple of museums. Tea is served with sandwiches, fruit and scones.

Jefferson Hotel, *16th & M Sts. NW, DC, 202.347.2200, 3-5pm every day.* The place to relax on tall armchairs, overstuffed sofas and down-stuffed pillows in front of a fire. Tea is served with sandwiches, scones and pastries in the lounge near the fireplace. One of the nicest tea times in DC.

Mayflower, *1127 Conn. Ave. NW, DC, 202.347.3000, 3-5pm M-Sat.* The Mayflower is alive with trees and pastries that jump out and seem say "dig in." Tea is served with scones and banana bread in the cafe promenade. The Mayflower has been doing this for years and business gets particularly busy on Saturdays.

Park Hyatt, *24th and M Sts. NW, DC, 202.789.1234, 3-5pm Th.-Sun.* The service and tradition at the Park Hyatt are what makes tea time here so special. Two different types of teas are served, both English (one is a full tea, and the other with champagne becomes a "Queen's Cocktail"), and always with scones. Reservations are required.

The Willard, *1401 Penn. Ave. NW, DC, 202.628.9100, 3-5pm M-F, 2:30-4pm Sat.-Sun.* Tea is served in the Willard Room on the weekends, in the cafe the rest of the week and always with sandwiches and pastries.

Chowin' Down in DC Museums:
Food with culture

Tourists come to DC to visit the museums and gawk. Residents and visitors need another reason to do the same. Besides, let's face it, suburbinites aren't eager to be seek walkin' around the Mall and gawking with a camera wrapped around their necks. So, here is a legitimate excuse for all of Virginia and Maryland to visit DC: the museums in the capital prepare some of the tastiest meals in the city.

National Gallery of Art, *Concourse level, 600 Const. Ave. NE, DC, 202.842.6191.* Is it a café on a busy street or an underground passageway illuminated by a faux waterfall and big skylight? No matter. Most meals are light, mid-priced and colorful. The West Building of the NGA has food stops, too.

National Museum of American History, Main Street Cafe, *14th St. & Const. Ave. NW, DC, lunch and dinner, 10am-5pm;* **Palm Court,** *11am-4pm, formal dining.* They serve — surprise! — American food here, so arrive with a pang for hot dogs, ice cream and fried chicken. There's also a soda bar that serves everything that the corner drug store could make: shakes, root beer floats and even birch beer.

National Air and Space Museum, Wright Place, *6th & Independence Ave. SW, DC, 202.371.8777, reservation required, lunch and dinner served;* **Flight Line,** *Continental Breakfast, lunch and dinner.* The Air and Space Museum emphasizes the ambience of life in orbit (lots of open space) rather than the details (steak in a tube, freeze dried ice cream). In fact, you really have to struggle here to find a connection between the restaurant and the museum (although, in all fairness, the restaurant seems to use the same brand of aluminum foil that the Space Lab is wrapped in. Is it a coincidence?).

Going to Court, Capital Style:
DC's court system

R eal things happen in DC, even though it would
sometimes seem that most events only occur on
TV or in the newspaper, and that actors and reporters
outnumber the rest of us. DC area courtrooms, however, are the setting for real local action (or, at least,
its consequences) with genuine criminals, self-serv-
ing attorneys and famous, honorable judges. Yes, as
any newspaperman can attest to, a courtroom is
where real news is made. If you're able to cope with
the fact that unsavory types like murderers, thugs,
bad lawyers and other criminals are in your midst as
they are being sentenced, tried or forced to work long
weeks at huge hourly rates, the courts offer free and
occasionally exciting shows.

Superior Court, *500 Indiana Ave. NW, DC, 202.
879.1010.* All cases except juvenile trials are open
to the public. The second and third floors have
criminal cases, while domestic violence is on the
first floor. A list of cases to be heard each day are
posted on individual courtroom doors. The courthouse gets empty around lunchtime, so come early
or late in the day.

US Federal Courthouse, *333 Constitution Ave. NW,
DC, 9-4pm M-F, 202.273.0555.* Cases are posted
on courtroom doors and are heard most days of
the week. This courthouse houses both the DC federal district courts and the DC Court of Appeals.

Supreme Court, *First St. NE, DC, 20543, 202.
479.3000.* Reservations are available, so write prior
to visiting if possible. Otherwise, call to find out
when arguments are scheduled—most are held
on Mondays and Wednesdays, not every week.
When cases are argued, two entrance lines form
at the court, one for limited seats to view the entire argument and another for 3 minute viewing.
Seating begins at 9:30am. In addition to the arguments, there are always two exhibits downstairs,
including a permanent one about the architecture
of the court, open 9am-4:25pm M-F.

DC Universities:
Culture on a student's wages

L ocal universities play host to everything literary, musical and otherwise cultural that the area offers. And, without Hollywood stars on the bill, tickets to university-related events are almost always affordable. Here are some contacts at local universities:

Gallaudet University, *800 Florida Ave. NE, DC, 202. 651.5501.* Call the theatre arts department.

George Mason University, *4400 University Dr., Fairfax, VA, 703.993.8888.* Ask for the Center for the Arts, which hosts films and theater.

Georgetown University, *37th & O Sts. NW, DC, 202. 687.3838.* Call to be placed on the mailing list of the Performing Arts office.

George Washington University, *800 21st St. NW, 202.994.1500,* has a concert and information hotline with upcoming events.

University of Maryland, *College Park, MD, 301. 405.2201 or 301.314.HOFF* has plays, musicals and movies.

EVENINGS AND SPECIAL EVENTS

Literary Readings:
Tea with an author

D C is packed with lawyers, politicians and writers. Since you have to pay a lawyer to talk and because nobody wants to hear what a politician has to say, why not spend the evening with a writer reading his or her book? Bookstores, university auditoriums and other public venues host literary readings that are usually open to the public and are free.

Chapters Bookstore, *1512 K St. NW, DC, 202. 347.5495,* hosts different types of readings including a lot of fiction, literary biography and big political books. Events about Proust and George Elliot are frequent topics, too. Readings begin at 7pm, seating is for 45 and tea is served.

Politics and Prose Bookstore, *5015 Conn. Ave. NW, 202.364.1919,* has readings almost every day, mostly fiction and local authors. The action starts at 7pm in the coffee house downstairs.

Smithsonian Resident Associate Program, *202. 357.3030,* hosts lectures and book signings by authors. Call for a schedule and to register.

Library of Congress, *101 Independence Ave. SE, 202. 707.5394,* has a fall and spring reading series. Call for a flyer.

Folger Shakespeare Library Evening Poetry Series, *20 3rd St. SE, DC, 202.544.7077,* hosts discussions with the actors.

Learning Capital Classics:
Symphonies in and nearby DC

Mozart and Old Europe speak through the instruments and symphonies in the area. You'd never know it, though, or appreciate a single crescendo unless you learn a little bit about classical music. And what better place to do it than with a local, public symphony or via an evening class.

Alexandria Symphony, *1900 N. Beauregard St., Alexandria, VA, 703.548.0085,* hosts concerts with local musicians in the orchestra. Call for a brochure with activities.

Fairfax Symphony, *Fairfax, 4024 Hummer Rd., Annandale, VA, 703.642.7200.*

Folger Concert Series, *201 E. Capitol St. SE, DC, 544.7077,* features renaissance music and period instruments. The first concert in each series has a pre-concert discussion, usually held on Fridays.

National Symphony Orchestra, *2625 Conn. Ave. NW, DC, Kennedy Center, 202.797.0083.* The NSO's education department hosts discussions with musicians and sometimes even with the conductors.

DC in the Stars:
Telescopic capital

Telescopes that peer into the heavens are a healthy reminder for people from the nation's capital that we're hardly at the center of the universe. So, for those who would confuse the belts around Saturn with, say, the beltway, we say: peer outward! Local astronomical organizations have the equipment and expertise to explain what you're looking at, and they are a great excuse to take an evening drive away from the flood lights of a major city like DC to a remote and quiet hillside to view the stars, search for comets or otherwise watch the universe speed by.

National Capital Astronomers, *301.320.3621,* has many professional astronomers among its 200 members who give monthly lectures, publish a monthly newsletter and sponsor trips during the summer to sites. Call to be placed on their mailing list.

Albert Einstein Planetarium, *National Air and Space Museum, 6th & Independence SW, DC, 202. 357.2700.* The Planetarium hosts regular shows about the search for extraterrestrial life.

Arlington Planetarium, *Arlington, VA, 703.358.6070.*

Rock Creek Nature Center, *5200 Glover Rd. NW, DC, 202.426.6829,* hosts after school programs on Wednesdays and weekends. Stargazing programs are occasionally held in conjunction with local astronomy clubs. Call for a listing of monthly programs.

DC Auctions:
Looking for the highest bidder

W here should you go to find a second hand sofa and to get excited about the purchase? An auction, of course, where hard-to-find antiques are offered side by side with other curios that might catch your fancy. Along the way it is possible to get a bargain or two, but only if you know what you're looking for before you go!

Laws Auction, *7209 Centreville Rd., Manassas, VA, 703.361.3148 or 703.631.0590,* is held every weekend of the year, F-Sun. Auctions are of two types: general and estate. In estate auctions, full houses are shipped to the auction table room by room.

All the World's a Fair:
DC fair-going

When the county fair provide a stage for the high school band to strike up a tune, it is time to find a free weekend, skip breakfast and search for the crowds. Crowds will be there, too, and that means action, rides and fun.

MARYLAND
Garret County Agriculture Fair, *Garret Henry Fair Grounds, MD, 301.334.1948,* August, week long.

Montgomery County Fair, *Montgomery County Fairgrounds, Gaithersburg, MD, 301.926.3100,* August, week long.

Maryland State Fair, *Timonium, MD, 410.252.0200.*

Great Frederick Fair, *Frederick, MD, 301.663.5895,* September, 8 days long.

Anne Arundal County Fair, *Crownsville, MD, 410. 923.3400.*

Charles County Fair, *La Plata, MD, 301.932.1234.*

St. Mary's County Fair, *Leonardstown, MD, 301. 475.2707,* September, 3 days long.

VIRGINIA
Prince William County Fair, *Manassas, VA, 703. 368.0173.*

Rockingham County Fair, *Harrisonburg, VA 540. 434.0005,* August, 6 days long.

Shenandoah County Fair, *Woodstock, VA, 703. 459.3867.*

WEST VIRGINIA
West Virginia State Fair, *Fairlea, WV 304.645.1090,* August, 8 days long.

Piano Bars Around DC:
Capital sing-alongs

W hy pay lotsa money for a beer on tap to the tune of recorded music when there are local taverns that give you the stage to belt out a tune? Try a piano bar, meet other good voices and join in as one of the area's bar room sing-alongs gets going, usually to the tune of old music and a live piano. Even if the alcohol doesn't actually help your singing, at the very least it will make you believe that you sing well, and that's what it is all about.

Fish Market, *105 King St., Alexandria, VA, 703. 836.5676, 8pm-1am Th.-Sat., $3 cover charge.* Darryl Ott has been playing ragtime sing-alongs here for 20 years.

Flaming Pit, *18701 N. Frederick Rd., Gaithersburg, MD, 301.977.0700, 8:30pm every night of the week.* Many local theatrical groups perform here and audience participation is encouraged.

James III Pavilion Hotel, *5901 Montrose Rd., Rockville, MD, 301.881.1100, Tu., Th., F, Sat.* Held in a Victorian, oak-paneled room, most songs are sing-alongs and audience participation is encouraged. Guest musicians perform on Friday night.

Mr. Smith's, *3104 M St. NW, DC, 202.333.3104, every night of the week.* Mr. Smith's is a casual piano bar where patrons sit on stools around the piano, drink and occasionally chime in.

Steeplechase Races:
A day with the horses

Horse racing and a family picnic go hand in hand if you skip the racetrack and head for the country and to a steeplechase race instead. Most steeplechases are held at large stables that are temporarily open to the public and all are full day events, best enjoyed with a few dozen sodas, lunch meat and family or friends. Don't forget to bring a pair of binoculars so you'll be able to follow the horses after they head for the hills.

Oatlands Point to Point, *Leesburg, VA, 703.777.9519.*

Fairfax Hunt, *Leesburg, VA, 703.532.2257 or 540. 882.4043,* has been run annually since 1939. There is a point-to-point race in the Spring and a steeplechase in September.

Middleburg Spring Races, *Middleburg, VA, 540. 687.6545, third weekend in April.* The Middleburg Races run six races and offer a $100,000 purse. Proceeds benefit the local hospital center and as many as 10,000 people have been known to show up on race day.

Foxfield Spring Races, *Charlottesville, VA, 804. 293.9501.* Compete with the crowds of students from the University of Virginia for space and attention. Dress nicely or take cover. Go Hoos!

Virginia Gold Cup Races, *The Plains, VA, 540. 347.2612.* The one-day long Virginia Gold Cup steeplechase race is held on the first Saturday in May. Advance ticket purchase is required.

GROUPS AND SPORTS

DC on the Links:
Where to get teed off

D C area greens are a more pleasant vista than the pavement of the Beltway. Fortunately, there are plenty of quality public golf courses in the area. Here are some of the best and least expensive:

MARYLAND

Enterprise, *2802 Enterprise Rd., Mitchellville, MD, 301.249.9220.* Enterprise is one of the area's nicest and is covered with azaleas at every turn.

Northwest Park Golf Course, *15701 Layhill Rd., Silver Spring, Wheaton, MD, 301.598.6100.* Northwest gets a lot of traffic, but it is so long (more than 7,000 yards) that the fairways don't often get backed up.

Little Bennet, *25900 Prescott Rd., Clarksburg, MD, 301.253.1515.* Little Bennet is set on a old dairy farm and shares space with fields of wildflowers. The course is very hilly, long and has a lot of blind shots and tricky par 3s.

University of Maryland Golf Course, *Northwest Quad, College Park, MD, 301.403.4299.* Although this is the University's hang-out, the long par 4s and the lake make this course amongst the most scenic in the area. You can hit a driver off every tee. There are no paralleling fairways, trees are situated between every hole and the course was built to co-exist with the local geography.

Redgate Golf Course, *14500 Avery Rd., Rockville, MD, 301.309.3055.* Redgate is hilly and a bit short but memorable for its carefully manicured greens. There are many blind shots that cause trouble for people who don't drive straight. There isn't a flat green on the course.

VIRGINIA

Pohick Bay Regional Golf Course, *10301 Gunston Rd., Lorton, VA, 703.339.8585.* Pohick is off the golfer beaten path and that means that its thin, hilly fairways are usually in good shape. More difficult than other local courses, with many doglegs and invisible greens, Pohick is rated as one of the ten most difficult public courses in the state.

Algonkian Regional Park Golf Course, *1600 Potomac View Rd., Sterling, VA, 703.450.4655.* Algonkian is known for its back nine, where drivers and long irons see action. It is very flat, maintains inexpensive course fees and is usually in good shape.

Digging Up DC:
Opportunities for budding archaeologists

The DC area was settled early by European explorers and for many millennium before that Native Americans inhabited the area. The result is an odd but exciting combination of archaeological sites and opportunities for anyone interested in participating in a dig.

Historic Annapolis Foundation, *186 Prince George St., Annapolis, MD, 410.269.0432,* has an archaeology lab and does field school with U of MD. Volunteers are asked to sort dirt and consult with archaeologists when something unexpected appears.

Center for Urban Archaeology for City Life Museum, *800 E Lombard St., Baltimore, MD, 410.396.3523,* sometimes has hands-on work for newcomers. They also accept volunteers for work around the museum.

Fairfax County Archaeological Services, *Falls Church, VA, 703.237.4881.*

Mountain Bikin' DC:
Two wheeling in capital dirt

M ountain bicycling can be a great way to explore some of the local parks at a faster pace than hiking. Many of the trails that once received horse traffic can handle mountain bicyclists, although the local authorities sometimes impose a fee to cover the costs of keeping up with the wear and tear of two-wheeled traffic.

WASHINGTON DC

Fort Dupont, *Minnesota & Mass. Aves. at Randle Circle SE, DC, 202.426.7723,* has 4.5 miles of trails.

MARYLAND

Black Hills Regional Park, *Boyds, MD, 301.972.9396.* Black Hills has trails best suited for horses, but adequate for mountain bikes. In addition, there is a visitors center and boating, fishing and picnic facilities.

C&O Canal, *just north of Great Falls, MD, 301. 299.3613,* has some toe paths that double as bike paths. Reconstruction from floods may interfere with a ride, so call first. Water pumps are turned off during winter and camping facilities are closed.

Lake Needwood, *Rock Creek Regional Park, Muncaster Mill Rd. & Avery Rd., Rockville, MD, 301. 762.1888,* has a two-mile dirt road around the lake and a paved biking trail that leaves from the No. 1 Picnic Area.

Patuxant River Park, *Upper Marlboro, Croom Airport Rd., near MD Rte. 382, 301.627.6074.* Patuxant has eight miles of horse trails that double as bike paths, although boardwalks are restricted to pedestrians only. All paths are unpaved and county residents get a break on the admission fee.

VIRGINIA

Fountainhead Regional Park, *VA, 703.250.9124,* has a four mile loop trail open to mountain bikers, but the other trails are only open to horseback riders and hikers.

Great Falls Virginia, *at Rte. 193 & Old Dominion Rd., McLean, VA, 703.285.2965,* has a few roads that are just for bikers. Half of the 15 miles of trails are open for mountain bikes, including all of the fire access and sandy gravel roads, through wooded area mostly. Pick up a trail map at the visitors center.

Lake Accontik, *5B exit off of 395 south to Braddock Rd., VA, 703.569.3464,* has a five mile gravel road that circles the lake. Think about bringing along a fishing rod.

Prince William Forest Park, *exit 50B off I-95 south, VA, 703.221.7181,* has about 11 miles of fire roads that are open for mountain bicycling. Mountain bikers are charged a fee to use the park. Be sure to pick up a brochure with a trail map at the visitors center.

W&OD, *from Shirlington to Percerville, VA, 703. 729.0596,* has a multi-use trail 45 miles long with asphalt and crushed gravel paved along an abandoned railroad bed. Trail guides are available along the route.

Capital Rock Climbing:
Vertical DC

F alling off a 125 foot cliff can be fun…if you're attached to a very thick rope. Indeed, rappelling is
the art of falling under control and overcoming fears.
It is also an increasingly popular sport with local en-
thusiasts, not all of whom are as fit as Spiderman or
can fly like Superman. Some do it during lunchtime
on the Virginia side of Great Falls (they call it "flash
climbing"); others do it by planning many months
ahead, with the help of a local rock climbing club.
Most rock climbing experiences begin with a classroom lesson on how to do it safely. After that, it is up
to you and gravity to get it right.

Potomac Appalachian Trail Club, *Mountaineering
Section, 703.242.0315.* Call for information, activities and events.

Seneca Rocks Climbing School, *Seneca Rocks, WV,
304.567.2600.* Call for information and good rates.

Breathing Under Water:
Scuba diving near DC

A hobby like stamp collecting may be cheaper, but it takes the excuse of a scuba diving expedition to travel to deserted beaches in exotic countries just to give the equipment a test run. First, though, you have to get certified and fortunately there are a handful of places around DC that will do that. After that, there are enough quarries and sunken ships in the area to keep most divers busy until they can land a good deal for a flight to a beach in paradise.

Northern Virginia Dive Club, *11751 Mossy Creek Ln., Reston, VA, 703.391.0547.*

Learning to Dance in DC:
From ballet to tap

Dance is exercise and exercise is the cure for 40 hours a week of DC desk stress. So, at age 8 or 80, tapping to the tune of the Cotton Club or bouncing in bare feet to the rhythm of modern dance music, dance and dance classes are for everyone. And, with a little sweat and without the tug of a tie, dance class is an easy way to meet people.

Academy of the Theatrical Arts, *1747 Conn. Ave. NW, DC, 202.462.2266,* offers drop-in lessons for ballet, tap and jazz.

Academy of the Maryland Youth Ballet, *7649 Old Georgetown Rd., Bethesda, MD, 301.652.2232,* has an extensive program of classical ballet and modern dance classes for adults and children. The teachers are experienced and the facility has plenty of space for practicing.

Dance Exchange, *7300 MacArthur Blvd., Glen Echo, MD, 202.229.6022,* is held in the Glen Echo Park and is sponsored by the National Park Service. Lessons are offered for most dance techniques and are limited in size.

The Dance Place, *225 8th St. NW, DC, 202.269.1600,* is a local center for the instruction of modern dance, but offers an array of adult classes in other forms, including African dance, pilates body conditioning and Latin ballroom dance. There's also a theater with performances every weekend.

Feet First, *7649 Old Georgetown Rd., Bethesda, MD, 301.656.9076,* offers classes in jazz, tap, modern and fitness dance for adults, plus classes for children. This is a non-profit organization and classes are taught by local professionals, some who run their own companies.

Ultimate DC:
Frisbee football

Frisbees may seem to be for kids, but Ultimate Frisbee is dirty, exhausting and competitive. Ultimate is a non-contact sport which requires some skills (throwing forehand, mostly), practice and strategy that have a short learning curve. But, the game is the ultimate (hah!) team sport, and anyone sitting out a game will gladly tell you everything you need to know to join in.

Washington Area Frisbee Club, *301.588.2629,* has team play and even tournaments. Call for locations, times of games, newsletter and other information (including parties).

DC's Winter Olympics:
Cold capital sports

E veryone else travels to the gym in the wintertime, or heads to the slopes. How, then, does the
US ever attract enough Americans to participate in
those bizarre winter olympic sports, and where do
they practice? In DC, of course. Curling, speed skating
and orienteering are decidedly cold weather sports,
and local venues attract DC's best cold weather athletes.

CURLING
This British sport is a cross between shuffleboard and
bowling and is a decidedly open event: men, women,
old, young, in-shape and not-in-shape athletes can participate, often with equal success. Local curlers are
usually glad to explain the rules and the 42 pound
rocks they use thankfully come with handles attached.
Call before you go to learn what clothing to wear.

Potomac Curling Club, *Cabin John Regional Park
Ice Rink, VA, 703.370.66282,* has sessions on Mon-
day evenings, 8-11pm. New members are welcome
anytime to watch or even participate on a team,
just as long as they are dressed warm and wear
rubber-soled shoes.

SPEED SKATING
Eric Heiden is an American speedskating legend,
even though few Americans know anything about
the sport. It is big news in the Netherlands, though,
and is a superb thigh exercise and a natural way to
get some speed, speed, speed.

Gardens Ice House, *Laurel Ice Arena, 13800 Old
Gunpowder Rd., Laurel, MD, 301.953.0100.* Speed
skating groups practice on Mondays and Wednesday evenings.

ORIENTEERING

As anyone who has seen it can attest to, orienteering is a vicious cross between navigating and running a marathon. The idea is to run through a course in a wooded area faster than the competition by avoiding natural obstacles, like rivers and shrubs. Even if you don't win or particularly like to read maps, it is a good excuse to take a vigorous, well organized hike that you will never forget!

Quantico Orienteering Club, *VA, 703.528.4636.*
Events are held throughout the year, usually twice each month on Sunday afternoons. Newcomers are welcome, and most events have four levels for all abilities. Just announce yourself as a first timer and dress according to the weather. Call the club hotline for upcoming events and directions.

DC Running Clubs:
Jogging for fun

Running is good exercise, no doubt, and doing it regularly makes you feel better. But, it can also be downright boring if you do it alone. And, if you do it without the right equipment and warm-up routine, it can be perilous. DC area running clubs offer potential running partners, information about the best routes and good advice on the equipment you need to do it right. In addition, most hold regular meeting and some even sponsor a series of races.

Montgomery County Road Runners Club, *MD, 301.353.0200,* has more than 3,000 members. The club organizes training runs and groups of runners for companionship on the pavement. The club information line has details about races, workouts and events.

Annapolis Striders, *MD, 410.268.1165.* The hotline gives details about races and other events.

Potomac Valley Track Club, *VA, 703.941.4317 or 703.671.2520,* The club hosts a series of races and other events throughout the year. Call for the monthly newsletter.

Capital Triathlons:
DC's ironmen and ironwomen

So, you're a runner. So, you like to swim. So, you're a biker. But, can you do a triathlon? If exercise is more than just an escape from beltway traffic and if you've ever glared in envy at the ragged few who travel to Hawaii and call themselves Iron men and women, DC offers you something almost as good: genuine triathlons with fewer miles to swim, run and bike. And, best of all, anyone can participate. Just remember, however, that there is still another mile to go!

Bud Light Triathlon Series, *Baltimore, MD,* usually in late June. 1.5K swimming, 40K bicycling, 10K running.

Make a Wish Triathlon, *Bethany Beach, DE,* usually in September. 1.5K swimming, 36K bicycling, 10K running.

Continental United States Ultra Triathlon, usually in October. 2.4 mile swimming, 112 mile bike, 26.2 mile run.

Sailing the Potomac:
Skirting the capital winds

I f the British were able to figure out how to sail a boat clear across the Atlantic and right up the Potomac before anyone had bothered to invent the ice cooler and potato chips, there's reason to believe that the rest of us can figure out how to do it today. Take a lesson, rent a sail boat or a windsurfer for the day and look out for the Key Bridge pylons.

Belle Haven Marina, *Alexandria, VA, 703.768.0018,* has a two day, 10-hour learn-to-sail course, with three persons to a class and a boat.

Washington Sailing Marina, *1 Marina Dr., Alexandria, VA, 703.548.9027,* has two six hour sessions on weekends. Registration includes a rental boat.

US Coast Guard, *2100 2nd St. SW, DC, 202. 267.1077,* offers classes in boating safety.

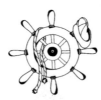

Hang Gliding Near the District:
Hanging in the wind

Planes are too expensive to learn to fly, bicycles don't get enough lift or speed, and with running the scenery doesn't pass, well, fast enough. Enter hang gliding, a baby boomer generation sport popularized in the early 1980s in Australia and on the dunes of Jockey's Ridge State Park in Nags Head, North Carolina. There are a few ways to be launched into the air on a hang glider: with an expert, behind a boat or off a sand dune or mountain. There are other important terms, like D-ring, and techniques to learn, but otherwise it is something that anyone can learn to do, at least for a day.

Kitty Hawk Kites, *Nags Head, NC, 919.441.4124.*
Call to make a reservation. Beginning lessons include films, ground school and five flights off the sand dunes.

Skateboarding on the Capital:
DC on a board

They sound like a freight train grinding its wheels on polished marble. They defy gravity, balance and signs which declare "No Skateboarding" but which have been quietly plastered over with stickers proclaiming, "Life, Liberty and My Skateboard." Skateboarding started in California, angers old ladies and if you have any balance and a decent board is a heck of a lot of fun.

Cedar Crest Country Club, *16850 Sudley Rd., Centreville, VA, 703.631.9362.* This is one of the area's premier skateboarding locales. There is a big ramp with a roof that makes it possible to skate as long as it isn't too cold. Helmet and pads are required.

Lansdowne, *Bero Rd., south of Baltimore. Take 95 north to 695 south to Hillns Ferry Rd. toward Lansdowne, MD.* This bowl has been abandoned by everyone except local skateboarders. The area isn't too nice, so it is a good idea to travel to Lansdowne in a group.

Capital Homes and Gardens:
House tours near DC

I t may be acceptable to stare at and dream about
some of the houses in Northwest DC or Potomac,
but it is far more satisfying to visit. And, why not? In
the name of charity and mother nature, a handful of
homeowners in the area with the best gardens open
their doors to the public for home and garden tours.

VIRGINIA
The Commonwealth of Virginia, *on the last full
week in April, 804.644.7776,* organizes garden and
house tours through local garden clubs, who in
turn contact private homeowners to request per-
mission to let the public through for one very special and colorful day. More than 30 cities throughout Virginia participate, including Alexandria,
Arlington, Leesburg, Warrenton, Winchester and
Warren County. Proceeds go to the restoration of
the grounds of historic landmarks in Virginia. Call
for a schedule and additional information about
other garden tours in the state.

MARYLAND
Held weekends in late April and May, 301.821.6933.
Call for a tour book with a map and a description
of the houses on the tour. Six counties in Maryland
participate. The tour has been held for more than
60 years and tour proceeds go to preserving the
state's historic properties. Houses are selected by
local historical societies or garden clubs.

Cross Country Skiing:
Not everything is downhill from here

L ift lines and gravity may have difficulty compet-
ing with the gentle, almost mesmerizing silence
of a snow filled forest with tree branches bent down-
ward and the moon's reflection mirrored in the bark.
Cross country skiing is also cheaper than downhill
skiing and after a good snowfall it isn't necessary to
travel very far to find good tracks. Some contacts:

River & Trail Outfitters, *604 Valley Rd., Knoxville,
MD, 301.695.5177,* runs tours and instructions,
with equipment included. Groups go out most
weekends between January and March when
there is snow on the ground. Groups head to
Cumberland, MD and Black Water Falls in West
Virginia.

Washington Ski Club, *VA, 703.536.8273.* Call the
action line for information about activities and
monthly meeting (and happy hour get togethers!).

DC Table Tennis:
To ping and to pong

D C has become something of a US haven for up-and-coming table tennis, nay Ping Pong, players. With the legitimacy of an Olympic medal awarded to its best players in years past, DC has sprouted a few ping pong clubs with all the amenities that table tennis players could want: tables, nets and balls.

Potomac Table Tennis Club, *Potomac Community Center, 11315 Falls Rd., Potomac, MD, 301. 983.4471.* Members of all skill levels practice on Tuesdays and Saturdays. Visitors are welcome.

Rosemary Rec. Center, *Silver Spring, MD, 301. 588.7051, 12-3pm M, W, 7-9pm W.* Most games are between area senior citizens who come regularly, but activities are open to everyone.

Recording Music in DC:
Sounding it out

I f there aren't many huge bands that have evolved from DC clubs in recent years, it isn't because anyone here had difficulty finding a recording studio. There are plenty of recording studios—knobs, wires, computers and all—around the District, including many set in basements, and it isn't necessary to have a recording contract to reserve one for an afternoon.

Avalon, *4848 Battery Ln., Bethesda, MD, 301. 951.3900,* has an "at home" recording feeling, and there are usually other bands around.

Bias Recording Co, *5400 Carolina Pl., Springfield, VA, 703.941.3333, www.biasrecording.com,* has custom designed studios with API consoles and Ampex MM 1200 multitrax with Dolby SR.

Cue Recording, *109 Park Ave., Falls Church, VA, 703.532.9033,* has state of the art recording.

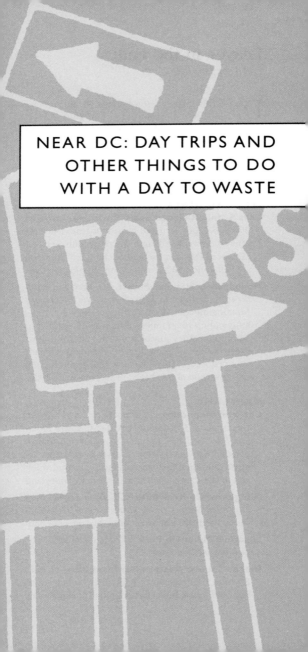

NEAR DC: DAY TRIPS AND OTHER THINGS TO DO WITH A DAY TO WASTE

Leaves in the Fall:
Gold in the fall

D C isn't the place to be when the Maple and Oak green slowly metamorphose into gold, orange, red and yellow. But, with many national parks, mountain ridges and, yes, trees in the vicinity, there's no need to travel far for colorful, seemingly endless Fall time panoramas. There are also some railroads that make special foliage trips for a few weeks each year.

WEST VIRGINIA

Cass Scenic Railroad State Park, *Seneca Rocks, 304.456.4300.* Two and four hour train rides are offered on weekends into the mountains between Memorial Day and the end of October. The trains are authentic coal burning 90-ton Shay locomotives.

Monongahela National Forest, *I-66 west, I-81 south, then the first exit to Rte. 55 west into Petersburg.* Monongahela in West Virginia, nearly 100 miles long and up to 50 miles wide, was devastated by our 18th century forebearers who chopped down every hardwood tree within reach but was remarkably restored to its native splendor when the federal government purchased the region in the 1920s.

MARYLAND

Catoctin Mountains, *I-270 north to US15 north to Cunningham Falls State Park and Catoctin Mountain Park, 301.271.3285 or 301.271.4432.* In addition to great views, Catoctin hosts an annual crafts, music and food festival during the second weekend of October each year in Thurmont, Maryland.

Alleghany Central Railroad, *from the Western Maryland Station in Cumberland, 800.TRAIN.50.* Three hour tours all week until the trees are bare.

Sugarloaf Mountain Park, *I-270 north to the Comus exit then west on Comus Rd.*

Garret County, Western Maryland, *301.334.1948.* Autumn Glory Festival in October includes a parade and a state high school football championship.

VIRGINIA

Skyline Drive, *I-66 West to Front Royal to 340 south.*
Great views all along the ridge, though it can get
packed with gawkers during weekends.

PENNSYLVANIA

Stewartstown Railroad, *on Rte. 851 east of I-81 be-*
tween Baltimore and York, 717.993.2936. Two foliage trips are offered every day for the duration
of the Fall season.

Learning to Fly Near DC:
The Mall from above

Learning to Fly is cheap, pilots don't have Beltway
bumper grind to worry about and much of the city
looks at least as nice from above as it does on ground
level. If watching others fly seems more secure, there
is a flying circus in the area.

Flying Circus Air Show, *Rte. 17, Bealeton, VA, 703-*
439.8661. The Flying Circus Air Show is held on
Sundays May through October. Rides are offered
after the show at a reasonable price, stomach turns
included.

Av-Ed Flight School, *8298 Old Courthouse Rd.,*
Leesburg Airport, Vienna, VA, 703.237.2565.
Offers intro flights.

ATC Flight Center, *10300 Glen Way, Ft. Washington,*
MD, 301.248.1480, offers intro flights for the
uninitiated, followed by ground school, practice in
the air and, eventually, an FAA private pilot exam.

Congressional, *7940 Airpark Rd., Montgomery Air-*
park, Gaithersburg, MD, 301.840.0880. Offers intro
flights.

Memorial DC:
National Cemetery

A rlington National Cemetery, VA, *703.545.6700.* Arlington Cemetery is the final place of rest for Americans from every corner of the country. The graves of four unknown soldiers are guarded there on a hilltop round the clock by an honor guard. President John F. Kennedy, his wife Jackie and his brother Robert are buried at ANC too, and most visitors travel to the cemetery to see these two sites.

Throughout the year, though, the cemetery sings with the daily ritual of tradition and maintenance. In late May, for instance, soldiers from the 3rd US infantry place small US flags in front of the more than 200,000 graves. Every morning, soldiers at the Tomb of the Unknown step through an elaborate, meticulously choreographed routine. The changing of the Tomb guard occurs every 30 minutes or 2 hours, depending upon the time of day.

Some sections, like 23 and 27 where black soldiers who fought for the country before the army was integrated are buried, are distinguished for the history they represent. Note also the high ground, where senior ranking officers are disproportionately represented, perhaps in a final effort to "pull rank."

Other sites to see include the mast of the USS Maine, the battleship whose destruction signaled the start of the Spanish-American war; a monument to and graves for the Americans who died in Beirut when a suicide bomber slammed into the US bunker there; the American soldiers killed in Iran in 1980 during an abortive effort to rescue the American hostages; and US astronauts killed when the Space Shuttle blew up and when the Apollo 1 capsule exploded during an abortive test run.

There are usually about 15 funeral processions every day at Arlington Cemetery. All members of the armed forces are entitled to be buried there with honors. The size and scope of the procession varies according to rank, but every funeral is accompanied by a bugler who plays taps, a firing party and a flag-draped casket. When generals are buried, canons are fired in their memory.

Barbecuing in DC:
Charcoal, hot dogs and beer

So, your apartment building doesn't allow you to barbecue on the balcony? That never stopped the Brits in 1812 when they razed the capitol, and it shouldn't be a hindrance to the rest of us. There are a handful of spots in DC that permit barbecuers to cook some up on the grill.

Fort Washington, *MD, 301.763.4600,* reserves grills. There's an 1820 fort that overlooks the Potomac, with fishing and even canon firings throughout the summer. Picnic tables and open areas are available, too. It is probably a good idea to come early to get the best site if you choose not to make reservations.

Fort Hunt or Rock Creek Park, *VA, 703.285.2601.* Grills can be reserved.

Galloping DC:
Going for a horse ride

It isn't necessary to build a stable, join the circus or fly out to the Midwest in order to go on a horse ride. The DC area is surrounded by countryside and horse trails that would make the Lone Ranger proud. Most places charge by the hour and require appointments to be arranged in advance.

Equestrian Enterprises, *966 Millwood Rd., Great Falls, VA, 703.759.2474,* has a small stable available for rides through Great Falls Park.

Corporate Cowboys, *Rte. 1, Hume, VA, 540-364.2627,* is situated in the Blue Ridge mountains on the 4,200 acre Marriot Ranch that hotel magnate J.W. Marriot used as a personal getaway. The Ranch has many miles of trails, most wide enough to ride a few horses abreast, and more than 200 horses suitable for all levels of riders.

Potomac Polo School, *Hughes & River Rds., Poolesville, MD, 301.972.7288.* Polo students can travel on 1,000 acres owned by the Muldoon family plus another 5,000 acres of public land nearby, which includes a part of the old C&O Canal towpath. The polo club is open to polo players.

Wheaton Regional Park Stables, *1101 Glenallen Ave., Wheaton, MD, 301.622.3311,* offers trail rides and riding lessons. They also maintain a course of jumps for more experienced riders.

Double SS Stables, *16211 McKendree Rd., Brandywine, MD, 301.372.8921,* is run by a couple of former government workers who decided to make a go of it with their first love: raising and riding horses. The handful of horses at Double SS have friendly, easy to remember names like Mork and Ajax, and experienced riders can ride unescorted.

Rock Creek Park Horse Center, *Military & Glover Rds. NW, DC, 202.362.0118,* is the Appalachian Mountains and a stable neatly rolled into the confines of Washington, DC. Trails lead through Rock

Creek, most riders are beginners and everyone is on the lookout for galloping VIP's who are thinking about their stables out west.

Wooden, Covered Bridges:
Scenes from a movie

In an age of eight-lane, steel bridges over massive rivers, there isn't much need for covered wooden bridges anymore, or much life left in the ones that are still around. Nonetheless, there are many of them nearby, silently awaiting clip-clop horse traffic or (aghast) even a car. Incredibly, more than 300 covered wooden bridges within a few hours of DC survive and function. Two good books about them are written by Richard Sanders Allens: *Covered Bridges of the Middle Atlantic States* (Stephen Greene Press, 1959) and *Covered Bridges of the Northeast* (Stephen Greene Press, 1974).

Local governments will also provide information to locate them. **Bucks County Tourist Commission,** *152 Swamp Rd., Doylestown, PA 18901, 215.345.4552;* **Lancaster County's Pennsylvania Dutch Convention and Visitors Bureau,** *501 Greenfield Rd., Lancaster, PA 17601, 717.299.8901;* **Frederick County Visitors Center,** *19 E. Church St., Frederick, MD, 301.663.8687;* **State of Virginia's Department of Economic Development,** *202 N 9th St., Ste. 500, Richmond, VA 23219, 804.786.4484;* **West Virginia's Department of Tourism,** *2101 Washington St. East, Bldg. 17, Charleston, WV 25305, 800.225.5982.*

Looking for George Washington:
Where he slept, how he lived

DC's namesake never saw a movie at the Uptown or had fries at Planet Hollywood, but he did make his way around town and to the neighboring states. He was well-known around town, too. In a city now possessed with a need to know where Washington (DC, that is) is day to day, there's a charm to figuring out where Washington (George) once was. Here's an incomplete list:

Washington's Birthplace, Virginia, *I-95 south to Rte. 17 east to Rte. 3 east to Washington's birthplace,* is where George was born. This Colonial farm, 40 miles east of Fredericksburg, is a slice of Williamsburg near DC, with restored homes, period costumes and exhibits about life in the 18th century.

Fredericksburg, Virginia is where Washington spent much time, usually visiting at his sister's mansion there but occasionally for the purpose of tossing a stone across the Potomac River. It is also where he threw a legendary silver dollar across the Rappahannock (not Potomac) River. Many buildings in town are associated with Washington, including Kenmore where his sister lived, the Mary Washington House that he bought for his mother and the Rising Sun Tavern built by his brother. Drop by the Visitors Center for information and addresses.

Alexandria, Virginia was something of a presidential pitstop for the nation's first commander-in-chief. Throughout Old Town Alexandria, many buildings commemorate visits by Washington, including the Ramsay House where George ate breakfast, the Stable-Leadbeater Apothecary Shop where the president bought some medicines and Gadsby's Tavern where Washington kicked back and sloshed down a cold one, or two. The Ramsay House is now Old Town's visitors' center and that's a good place to begin a tour.

Montpelier Mansion, *Montpelier Dr., Laurel, MD, 301.953.1376,* maintained by the State Capital Parks and Planning Commission, is where Washington recorded in his diary that he became ill during one of many stops to Montpelier. The Mansion is open for tours and programs all year, with festivals and events held from time to time. An art center is on the property, too.

Mount Vernon, *south of Alexandria, VA, 703.780.2000,* is where Washington lived, and his house has been fully restored. Mount Vernon is privately owned, but it is maintained like a state park.

Drag Racing Near DC:
10 seconds of zoom

A drag racing car can be anything from a souped-up Chevy to a custom built monster on wheels. The pits are accessible for a few extra dollars, the races are run non-stop all day long, engines boom and drivers and mechanics are glad to explain the intricacies of the sport even as they are preparing for the next go-around. There are eight tracks near DC that play host to car and motorcycle drag races between March and September. Where there's a waft of burning rubber, the potential for blowouts and, yes, crowds, crowds, crowds, it is likely there's a drag racing strip nearby.

Capitol Raceway, *1455 Jackson Rd., Rte. 3S south, Crofton, MD, 410.721.9664,* has races on Saturday.

Cecil County Raceway, *1575 Theodore Rd., Rising Sun, MD, 410.287.6280,* holds Friday evening and Sunday afternoon races.

Maryland International Raceway, *Rte. 234, Budds Creek, MD, 301.449.RACE,* is open on Saturdays.

Mason Dixon Dragway, *40 East Ave., Rte. 40, Hagerstown, MD, 301.791.5193,* runs Sunday races.

75/80 Dragway, *Rts. 75 & 80 intersection, Urbana, MD, 301.865.5102,* has Wednesday, Friday and Saturday races.

Colonial Beach Dragway, *Rte. 205, Colonial Beach, VA, 804.224.7455,* has Sunday races.

Old Dominion Speedway, *Rte. 234, Manassas, VA, 703.361.RACE,* has Friday night races.

Summerduck Dragway, *Rte. 17, Culpepper, VA, 703.439.8080,* has Saturday and Sunday races.

Summit Point Raceway, *Rte. 13, Summit Point, WV, 304.725.8444,* is the region's foremost racing site and has a full racing schedule throughout the summer.

Searching DC for Cool Rocks:
Capital fossils

If the District is a goldmine now for lobbyists and lawyers, then they should've visited a few millennium ago. Back then, the rivers were virtually oozing with gold nuggets, and there were some exciting shark teeth and fossils in the making nearby. Here are the places to pan and rock hunt:

Goldvein, Virginia, *12 miles west of I-95 at Fredericksburg,* was once the center of the region's gold mining effort, and 20 mines were operating all at once in the late 19th century. Now, it is a tiny town with little Mandy Lot Run Creek nearby, the local place to pan for the shiny stuff.

In the vicinity of Rosecroft Raceway, there are good spots to collect newly exposed fossils. The place to be is along the stream that runs through town, especially after a storm hits so the banks are exposed. *To get there, take Beltway exit 4A, then go to St. Barnabus Rd. south. Take a left on Brinkly Rd. after a quarter of a mile, then go to the Alpine Apartments sign past the Rosecroft entrance. The path on the right of Brinkly Rd. continues for about 100 yards to the stream.*

The shores of the Chesapeake Bay are lined with fossils of whales and plenty of ancient shark teeth, free for the person who finds them. A good place to search is the **Calvert Cliffs State Park,** *Brandywine, MD, 301.888.1410,* since the local marine museum staff can give provide directions to a good spot. The nearby **Calvert Marine Museum,** *Solomons, MD, 410.326.2042,* has a full display of local fossils, including a great white shark skeleton. There's a two mile trail from the parking lot to the Bay, so bring hiking shoes.

Cottages Near the District:
Better than a hotel

Why gaze longingly at a beautiful mansion set on a ranch while you're on your way to a 70-ish deco brick hotel for a vacation? Could it be that centralized A/C smells better than the aroma of farmlife? In any case, there are many cottages around the DC area that were once houses on plantations, built by foreign royalty as a nice getaway or created for some other reason, and many are available for weekend getaways. Bring a history book, some food to cook in the kitchen and a pair of tense shoulders to relax.

Welbourne, *Middleburg, VA, 540.687.3201,* has four cottages. Visitors can eat breakfast at the main mansion.

Blue Ridge Bed and Breakfast, *Flint Hill, VA, 540. 955.1246.* The main house at the Caledonia has been painstakingly restored over the past thirty years. Caledonia is situated in the Shenandoah Valley, close to Bryce Mountain Ski Resort and some Virginia vineyards.

Barley Sheaf Farm, *Newton, VA, 215.794.5104,* is a seemingly ancient plantation situated on 500 acres of farmland. At the turn of the century, the icehouse was enlarged and redecorated to serve as the guest cottage. The very large main mansion is available in addition to the cottage, which has a few guest rooms, too.

Locust Hill, *Charlottesville, VA, 804.979.7264,* is the birthplace of Merriweather Lewis, the explorer who teamed up with Clark to explore the wild west. The 18th century house has since been occupied by another family not related to Lewis, but the antiques and art are enough to send you back in time.

Coleman Cottage, *Greenwood, VA, 804.979.7264,* is situated on a family owned plantation right next to other old buildings that justify a trip in their own right. The 1840 mansion there is the main house on the land and has been occupied by the same

NEAR DC: DAY TRIPS   75

family for nearly 80 years. There's an 18th century tavern next door that served drinks to soldiers fighting in the French Indian War. And, there are gardens, a functioning six-sided icehouse, a smoke-house and a fully functional eight stall stable.

Wineries Around DC:
Capital cabernet

I n Virginia and Maryland, there are more wineries (50+) than there are varieties of wine in the most upscale supermarket. They aren't a new creation either, since both presidents George Washington and Thomas Jefferson wrote about them and, indeed, tried to make their own at their personal estates, albeit without much success. Most local wineries are open for tours and free tastings. For hours and locations write to:

Virginia Wine Marketing Program, *Virginia Department of Agriculture and Consumer Services, Division of Markets, PO Box 1163, Richmond, VA, 23209.*

Maryland Department of Agriculture, *Marketing Services, 50 Harry S Truman Pkwy., Annapolis, MD, 21401.*

Into DC Nature:
Local nature centers

A midst everything modern, one very exciting way to spend a day is at a nature center. Most are run by local governments and all are packed with critters, vegetation and everything else that lives in or around your back yard.

Rock Creek Nature Center, *5200 Glover Rd. NW, DC, 202.426.6829,* has the only planetarium in a national park and offers local self-guided tours. Rangers will occasionally take visitors out on a trail exhibition. There are also some nighttime trips to gaze out at the stars. Call for a monthly list of programs.

Prince William Forest Park Visitors Center, *Rte. 619, Triangle, VA, 703.221.7181,* has 35 miles of hiking trails in the vicinity. Biking is allowed on fire roads. There is a family camping ground and the environmental center hosts programs about the flora and fauna. Some 1930s vintage cabin camps of various sizes are available for rent, too.

Gulf Branch Nature Center, *Arlington, VA, 703. 358.3403,* sits on 50 acres of a valley. Located in a stream valley, the park has hiking trails that lead to the Potomac and environmental education programs. The Center has displays of wildlife and live reptiles to see and learn about, as well as a display about Native Americans.

Long Branch Nature Center, *Arlington, VA, 703. 358.6535,* has wooded trails that lead to Arlington's only swamp. There is a native plant garden and a children's garden, too.

Potomac Overlook Nature Center and Regional Park, *Arlington, VA, 703.528.5406,* has hiking trails and maintains a nearby archaeological dig. This 95-acre preserve has trail access to the Potomac River and is a lively forest surrounded by the din of urban life.

Hidden Oaks Nature Center, *4030 Hummer Rd., Annandale, VA, 703.941.1065,* on 52 acres has all types of live reptiles, environmental exhibits, programs and even ballfields.

Hidden Pond Nature Center, *8511 Greeley Blvd., Springfield, VA, 703.451.9588,* is a neighborhood nature center situated next to a two-acre man-made pond and is run by the Fairfax County Park Authority. Exhibits change with the seasons and according to animal life and cycles. Look for the frog and caterpillar displays, and consider taking a hike on the marked trails that lead throughout the park.

Walney Visitor Center, *5040 Walney Rd., Chantilly, VA, 703.631.0013,* is housed in a two hundred year old farmhouse on a 600+ acre park. The nature/ history park has a visitor center with snakes and other displays. The big attraction here is the more than five miles of trails which are easy to navigate with a trail map. This is a good place to go for a day-long walk.

Ramsey Nature Center, *Alexandria, VA, 703. 834.4829,* has a live honeybee colony and regular programs for children of all ages.

Clearwater Nature Center, *Clinton, MD, 301. 297.4575,* partially covered with lava rock, has an exhibit room with displays about Prince George County's natural history and exhibits with live animals. There's a 15 acre lake, good for fishing, within walking distance. The grounds have facilities for camping, baseball and tennis.

30th St. Nature Center, *Mt. Rainier, MD, 301. 927.2163,* explores nature as it exists in your back yard. This is the only nature center in an urban setting, and it is truly right in the community. The Center occasionally hosts field trips to teach children about the environment. Also offered are an astronomy program, adult outings to local sites, a bird watchers groups and craft workshops.

Watkins Nature Center, *Upper Marlboro, MD, 301. 249.6202,* has an indoor pond with some very large bullfrogs. There are also many user friendly, color coded trails, a puppet theater, a camp fire program, an exhibit on reptiles and an indoor pond.

Brookside Nature Center, *Wheaton, MD, 301. 946.9071.* Brookside has slimy, interesting creatures, including snakes, turtles and a variety of fish. In the kids' section you can smell and compare different types of commonly used herbs. Also, there are environment and crafts programs for children and a self-guided trail. Take a peek at the honeybee observation hive.

Meadowside Nature Center, *Rockville, MD, 301. 924.4141.* Meadowside has an indoor forest and a small pond and cave for kids to explore. Other exhibits feature a cave for children to crawl through, a display about Native Americans and plenty of live reptiles including snakes, turtles and other creatures. Also, take a look at the bird feeder in the back and the flying visitors who stop here.

Horse Racing Near the Capital:
A day with the horses

Horse racing in the area has a history older than the Republic itself (George Washington was a fan), and something of a tradition since the Pimlico hosts the Preakness Stakes, the second tier of the annual Triple Crown. Although local race tracks can get pretty smokey and there usually isn't any shortage of professional gamblers in the background, there is always plenty of space for young amateurs. Bring a ten spot, a small appetite and, if you have them, a pair of binoculars.

Pimlico Race Course, *Baltimore, MD, 410.542.9400,* is the nation's second oldest racetrack and is set right in the middle of Baltimore. Live races are held from April to June every year.

Laurel Race Course, *Laurel, MD, 301.725.0400,* owned by the same people who own Pimlico, runs all year round and has the best local thoroughbred racing. Group visits to the training facilities can be accommodated by the public relations department.

Charles Town, *Rte 340 N, WV, near Harpers Ferry, 304.725.7001.*

Rosecroft, *6336 Rosecroft Dr., Fort Washington, MD, 301.567.4000,* is the only harness racing track in the area. Races are held in the evening and at night.

Farmlife Near DC:
How to spend the weekend with a moo

Some people come to cities to escape farmlife while others seem to acknowledge that a city is filled with animals, albeit of a different variety. In any case, some local farms rent rooms to city folk who want to return to nature and get close with a farmer and his animals. If you go, remember to wear old shoes and watch where you step!

VIRGINIA

Caledonia Farm, *Flint Hill, VA, 703.675.3693,* set in the Blue Ridge Mountains, raises different varieties of beef cattle.

Jordan Hollow Farm, *next to Shenandoah National Park in Stanley, VA, 540.778.2285,* is a 150-acre colonial horse farm with 21 guest rooms, including a few with fireplace and bath. Horseback riding is offered.

Shenandoah Valley Farm and Inn, *McGaheysville, VA, 540.289.5402,* has fish ponds, a tennis court and black Angus cattle.

WEST VIRGINIA

Prospect Hill, *Gerrardstown, WV, 304.229.3346,* is a 225-acre farm with a big Georgian mansion right in the center.

Stonebrake Cottage, *Shepherdstown, WV, 304.876.6607,* has 10 acres of good hiking grounds, and the C&O Canal towpath is nearby.

PENNSYLVANIA

Meadow Spring Farm, *Kennet Square, PA, 610.444.3903,* is filled with cows and is beautifully situated in the middle of nowhere.

Beaver Creek Farm, *Strasburg, PA, 717.687.7745,* is situated near the Amish country on a chicken farm.

Buck Valley Ranch, *Warfordsburg, PA, 717.294.3759,* in the Appalachian mountains offers horse rides on its hilly terrain.

Cedar Hill Farm, *Mount Joy, PA, 717.653.4655,* offers rooms in an early 19th century farmhouse set in the middle of crops, lots of chickens and a chicken house. The owner, Mr. Swarr, has lived there all his life and has filled it with antiques.

Country Stay, *Mount Joy, PA, 717.367.5167,* is a 98-acre Mennonite farm set amidst cows, wheat, soybean and corn fields.

Maplewood Farm, *Gardenville, PA, 215.766.0477,* is a small farm with some rooms for rent, each filled with early 19th century antiques.

Pleasant Grove Farm, *near Lancaster in Peach Bottom, PA, 717.548.3100,* is a 168-acre working dairy farm situated around a very old country home. Candlelight breakfast is served here.

Whitehall Inn, *New Hope, PA, 215.598.7945,* is a 13-acre horse farm with a pool and tennis court. A four-course candlelight breakfast is served.

DC Berries:
Where to pick them wild and fresh

Skip the supermarket and head for the forests. After all, that's where all the good blackberries are and, besides, what's the fun of buying fresh fruit when it comes in plastic, anyhow? The pickin' is best between late May and early July.

Washington and Old Dominion (W&OD) Railroad, VA, *between Purceville and the Intersection of Rte. 7 & Rte. 9.* Stick to the trail and hop back into the car and head for another section of the trail if the pickin' gets light.

Pick Your Own DC Fruit:
Capital fruits

Strawberry patches smell so good that they seem almost, well, artificial. Fresh blackberries are so plump and delicate that they can barely survive the journey from vine to hand to mouth. Pick-your-own fruit orchards are an eat all you can event, with the added obligation that you buy some to eat at home. Expect new flavors, intoxicatingly fresh fruit aromas, a happily swelled belly, a little sunburn and a few pounds of bright greens, yellows and blues that aren't likely to survive a nighttime snack on the refrigerator shelf.

SEASONS
May: *Asparagus, 3 wks.* **June:** *Strawberries, 3 wks., Sour Cherries, 2wks.* **July:** *Raspberries, 3wks., Cherries, 2 wks., Blueberries, 4 wks., Blackberries, 3 wks., Peaches, 6 wks.* **August:** *Grapes, 3 wks.* **September:** *Apples, 4 wks.* **October:** *Pumpkins, 4 wks.*

MARYLAND
Calvert County
Seidel Farm, *1 hr. from DC, Huntingtown, 410. 535.2128,* blackberries, grapes.

Carrol County
Sewell's Farm, *90 min., Taneytown, 410.756.4397,* strawberries.

Frederick County
Pryor's Orchard, *90 min., Thurmont, 301.271.2693,* cherries, blueberries.

Glade Link Farms, *Walkersville, 301.898.7131,* fruits.

High Hopes, *Middletown, 301.371.6228,* fruits.

Harford County
Lohr's Orchard, *75 min., Churchville, 410.836.2783,* strawberries, cherries, peaches, green beans, tomatoes.

Hoopes Quaker Hill Farm, *Forrest Hill, 410. 838.5583,* fruits.

Howard County

Larriland Farm, *Woodbine, 410.442.2605,* strawberries.

Sharp Farm, *25 min., Glenwood, 301.489.4630,* pumpkins.

Montgomery County

Rock Hill Orchard, *50 min., Mt. Airy, 301.831.7427,* strawberries, sour cherries, snap peas, tomatoes, blackberries, raspberries, apples, pumpkins.

Butler's Orchard, *30 min., Germantown, 301. 972.3299,* strawberries.

Homestead Farm, *Seneca, 301.977.3761,* strawberries.

Prince George's County

Cherry Hill Farm, *25 min., Clinton, 301.292.4642,* strawberries, blackberries, peaches, apples, Halloween festival.

Darrow Berry Farm, *Glenn Dale, 301.390.6611,* pumpkins.

Johnson's Berry Farm, *Upper Marlboro, 301. 627.8316,* fruits.

Parker Farms, *Clinton, 301.292.3940,* fruits.

VIRGINIA

Caroline County

Snead's Asparagus Farm, *60 min., Fredericksburg, 540.371.9328,* asparagus.

Fairfax County

Hartland Orchard, *60 min., Markham, 540.364.2316,* cherries, peaches, apples.

Potomac Vegetable Farms, *Tysons Corner, 703. 759.2119,* fruits.

Westmoreland County

Westmoreland Berry Farm, *100 min., Oak Grove, 804.224.9171,* strawberries, red raspberries, black raspberries, blueberries, blackberries.

Mills Near the District:
Capital grind

With so many operating mills in the area, it is almost difficult to believe that the flour we buy was probably ground by an electric machine. Back in the 19th century when electricity was still an idea, mills were constructed in every village and town in America and everyone congregated there either to grind corn or wheat, or to buy some of the flour that was created in the process. River water, as any third grader can attest to, provided the power for the great shaft to turn and the grindstones inside the mill did the rest of the work. Flour purists and natural food types argue that the product of mills really does taste different than the generic electrically produced flour that is for sale at Giant, since the mill process doesn't remove the natural oils. Regardless, the generic stuff certainly doesn't come with a mill and a history attached, and that is reason enough to spend a day visiting a few mills.

DC

Pierce Mill, *Tilden St. at Beach Dr. in Rock Creek Park, 202.426.6908, 9am-5pm W-Sun.* This 170 year old mill is the last of the old, water-powered grist mills, one of nine that once existed along Rock Creek, and one of more than 20 that once functioned in DC. There is a movie to watch, three floors to roam, and a ranger on duty to explain everything.

MARYLAND

Union Mills Homestead and Grist Mill, *3311 Littlestown Pike, Rte. 97, Union Mills near Westminster, 410.848.2288, Noon-4pm Tu.-F in the spring and summer.* Run by a non-profit organization, the Homestead is a museum with a house open to the public. The 18th century grist mill has been owned and operated by a local family through six generations. It was reconstructed recently and it produces a variety of flour and buckwheat that are for sale there. There is also a blacksmith and grounds with gardens.

Wye Mill, *Rte. 662 in Wye Mill at the intersection of Rtes. 213, 404 and 662, just off Rte. 50, 410. 827.6909, 11am-4pm Sat.-Sun. in the summer.* Wye Mill has been in operation since 1670 and once helped ground flour that fed the troops of General George Washington while he was stationed at Valley Forge.

VIRGINIA

Burwell-Morgan Mill, *Rte. 255 in Millwood, between Middleburg and Winchester, 540.837.1799, W-Sun. in the summer.* The Burwell-Morgan Mill is new by mill-standards. It was constructed in the late 18th century by a family that fought in the American Revolution. A display inside explains the milling process.

George Washington's Grist Mill, *5514 Mt. Vernon Memorial Hwy., Rte. 235 off Rte. 1 in Alexandria, 703.780.3383 or 703.339.7265, 9am-5pm Th-M.* This mill was reconstructed from parts of mills that once served George Washington on the same site. It is now a state park.

Woodson's Mill, *Rte. 778 in Lowesville, 804.277.5604, mill is open Saturdays only but grounds are open every day.* Built in the late 18th century, there are two mills are in operation here. One grinds flour with two sets of stones and the other generates electricity. All types of flour are for sale at the shop.

Baltimore's Museum:
A capital neighbor

The Smithsonian is DC, but the Mall and its museums aren't the extent of the area's great educational visits. Indeed, Baltimore wasn't blessed with a Smithsonian benefactor, but it seems to have balanced the benefit of having avoided DC's bureaucratic gut with support from Annapolis and has established some exciting, not-to-be-found-inside-the-beltway museums that are snazzy enough to make even the Air and Space Museum blush.

Hackerman House, Walters Art Gallery, *600 N. Charles St., 410.547.9000.* This 1850 mansion houses one of the nation's finest displays of Asian art. The entire building was renovated in 1991 and was donated to the city to display the amazing and extensive 19th century collection of the Walters family.

Baltimore Museum of Industry, *1415 Key Hwy., 410.727.4808.* This is a learning museum with hands-on displays about shucking oysters, making cans and otherwise participating in the industry that contributed to Baltimore's growth way back when. Remember to ask when the auto assembly line will be operating, in case you want to buy a newly built car or if you just want to see how it works.

Maryland Science Museum, *Inner Harbor, 410.685.5225.* This is the ultimate learning experience, and practically every display is designed to use, touch, operate or otherwise be part of. This is science in motion with an Imax theater to boot.

Babe Ruth Museum, *216 Emory St., 410.727.1539.* Though Babe played in New York, he was originally a Baltimore native, and the city is proud of it especially when the Orioles aren't winning. This is where the Babe housed many of his treasures, and they are all on display.

B&O Museum, *901 W. Pratt St., 410.752.2388.* The 1850 building that houses the B&O Museum was the country's first train station. Now, it is a repository for the great engines that have served their purpose and can explain an exciting era in the development of a young nation.

International Partying in the Capital:
Multi-lingual fiestas

C ongress celebrates every couple years in November; the rest of us commonfolk Americans do it the 4th of July, Christmas and even Halloween. The rest of the world parties too, and since parties are fun and because so much of the rest of the world is here in DC, why not partake in the fun with them, especially if it fits conveniently into our own schedules? Here is a synopsis of when International DC parties and where:

Cherry Blossom Festival, *early April.* Washington loves its cherry blossom trees down near the Jefferson Memorial tidal basin, but so too do the Japanese, and for many more years than the rest of us. The Japanese have been picnicking, socializing and otherwise enjoying the blossoms since the 8th century in fact, though it has only been in the past half millennium that the custom spread to include everyone, both king and common man. DC hosts an annual cherry blossom parade down Constitution Avenue, and dancers and singers perform nearby.

Italian Republic Day, *June 2, 1946, call 202.638.1348 for information.* Every day is something of a celebration with the local Italian-American community, but Republic Day is particularly big. Casa Italiana, next to the Holy Rosary Church, is the local center for Italian culture, food and fun, and the festival, of course.

Sonnenwendfeier, *late June, Blob's Park, 8024 Max Blob's Rd., Jessup, MD, 410.799.0155.* The Germans celebrate the longest day of the year with a bonfire and a lot of sausage and beer

Bastille Day, *July 14.* The French romanticize revolution, but fortunately don't generally celebrate their festivals that way. The local French community does accept token gifts from the French Embassy, perhaps as a peaceable alternative to destroying the embassy outright. In addition, Dominique's Restaurant kicks in with sponsorship of a now-famous waiters' race in which all participants have to keep two small champagne bottles and two glasses upright while running a few miles. It is hard under the best of circumstances, but a real challenge when it rains. The embassy also hosts an event, *call 202.944.6064 for information. For information about other goings-on call Alliance Francaise, 202.234.7911 or www.afusa.org and Accueill at 202.944.6012.*

Capital Processed Food:
They make it, you eat it

F ood is as much of the capital culture as red tape. Fortunately, the DC area produces plenty of both and sometimes it is possible to see both being created. If it is food that you are after, with red tape gratuitously attached, consider taking a trip to one of the destinations below.

Herr's Snack Food, *2 hr. from DC, Nottingham, PA, 800.284.7488.* Herr's is the potato chip source, and its factory is a mecca for the junk food aficionado (read: everyone who watches TV for more than one hour each day). Herr's will show you the conveyor belts that carry slices of potato to the sizzling hot tubs of cottonseed oil. They taste even better hot off the belt than they do from an air-tight bag, so the trip is especially fulfilling on an empty stomach. Here's a hint about how to make the most of the trip: there is free food at the end!

David W Wehr's Seafood, *1 hr. from DC, Kent Island, MD, 410.643.5778.* You can consider the crab meat pickers on this tour to be pros at what they do all day long. Workers here sit at long tables with pointed knives in hand opening crab after crab so that by the end of the day each nets an amazing 400 pounds, in the process discarding nearly 4,000 crabs. All the more amazing, nobody here seems to sneak a free mouthful in between crabs and everyone works six days a week during the harvest season between May and November. Wehr's will steam up some crabs for you after the tour, since it is likely to make you hungry. Call first to let them schedule a tour and to learn when the local fishermen will be on site to discuss their work. Work continues in the wintertime with seafood shipped in from other parts of the country.

Moore's Candies, *45 min. from DC, 3004 Pinewood Ave., Baltimore, MD, 410.426.2705.* Not all good chocolate comes from Europe, fortunately, and some of the best is locally produced. Moore's is a family-owned business situated just north of Baltimore that makes hand made chocolates. The tour consists of whatever is being produced that day and a slide presentation if you ask for it. Inside are pounds and pounds of fudge, clean copper kettles and, yes, enough chocolate to fill the home of Willie Wonka. Free samples await at the end, in case you're hungry. Tours are offered on Tuesdays and Thursdays.

University of Maryland Apiary, *College Park, MD, 301.405.3913.* Bees outnumber students at the University of Maryland by a buzz. Actually, the numbers aren't even close, and since the nearly one million bees that live in glass hives and work during the warmer months at U of MD produce their delicious honey 24 hours a day for the duration of their existence, they may be more productive than the student body, too. The beehive tour starts in a classroom and you can watch as they remove raw honey from a hive. An instructor explains how pollen and propolis figure into the production process and, best of all, there are samples at the end! Tours are offered in spring and fall only, must be arranged in advance and are preferable in groups.

Government for Free:
Capital giveaways

The government is in debt, but we pay taxes. What gives and where does the cash flow? How about in the form of freebies from the federal government, like the ones below. Here are some ways to earn money back via entitlements after the government gets its share and before DC calculates its deductions.

National Archives, Genealogy Workshops, *Const. Ave. & 7th St. NW, DC, 202.501.5000.* The National Archives, repository to everything worth remembering that fits in file cabinets, has information about our ancestry and classes to instruct you how to go about a search.

National Archives, Newsreel Copies, *Const. Ave. & 7th St. NW, DC, 202.501.5000 or 301.713.7050 (all newsreels are kept at the new College Park, MD facility).* The government has a movie theater that is stocked and is free. The motion picture, sound and video branch of the National Archives has everything from government produced documentaries to Supreme Court arguments and news reels that date from the 20s. Since everything is in the public domain, you can copy anything you want if you come with a cassette or VHS tape.

US Botanic Garden Conservatory, Lunch Lectures, *front of the Capitol, 202.226.4082.* If you ever wanted to vegetate during lunch, this is definitely the place to do it. Lunchtime lectures here are mostly free, happen about one each month, feature the foremost authorities in the greenhouse world and are usually filled, especially in the wintertime.

US Capitol, Flags Flown Over The Capitol, *call your local congressman or congresswoman.* The average flag above the capitol flies for less than one minute. Why? Because anyone with an American flag is permitted the honor of flying their flag above the Capitol for free. Every year, nearly 150,000 flags are flown above the capitol, and each is rewarded with a certificate verifying the feat.

National Air and Space Museum, Science Demonstrations, *Sixth & Independence SW, DC, 202. 357.1300.* The "How Things Fly" gallery across from the amazing Langley Theater has science demonstrations everyday that cover explanations of the physics of flying. Best of all, since most adults don't know much more about these things than do their kids, students of all ages are welcome and encouraged to show up.

Federal Bureau of Prisons, Letters To Famous Prisoners, *202.307.3126.* The US prison system is loaded with celebrities. Chances are that they don't have much to do all day long and, best of all, they can't ask the telephone book people to hide their addresses. No guarantees, though, on a reply and don't bother asking what they have planned for the upcoming weekend.

White House, Free Birthday And Anniversary Cards, *White House Comment Office, 1600 Penn. Ave. NW, DC 20500.* Here's an entitlement for the average American: a right to a free birthday or anniversary card on age 80 or older or anniversary 50 and up. Requests should be sent a month in advance.

US Geological Survey, Satellite Images Of Your Home, *605.594.6151.* US satellites have taken photos of the entire country, including one of your very own home and neighborhood. They do it often, too, and don't charge very much for a black and white print. What a great way to welcome someone to the neighborhood!

NOTES

ORDERING INFORMATION

OYO titles are sold throughout the globe. If your local bookstore does not carry OYO guide books, please contact us for ordering information at the address below. If you would like to order more copies, individually or in bulk, please contact our distributors at the following phone numbers: National Book Network *1.800.462.6420,* Ingram *1.800.937.8200,* or Baker & Taylor *1.800.775.1800.*

ON YOUR OWN PUBLICATIONS
415 NW 21st Ave., #501
Portland, OR 97209
Tel/fax: 503.279.6400
email: OYOBOOKS@AOL.COM

THE OYO STORY

On Your Own, or OYO, is a child of the late 1980s and early 1990s, when travel to previously inaccessible places like eastern Europe, China and Russia finally became possible. During that time, Jeff Brauer, Julian Smith and Veronica Wiles headed off in different directions to explore the globe.

After traveling for months, all three returned with a love for the road and for the many people they met along the way. They realized, though, that despite their inquisitive wanderings they wanted to learn more about the places they visited. Soon, they soon decided to do something about it.

When Jeff returned from traveling to begin law school at the U of Virginia in 1992, he jump-started OYO with the help of other students. Julian joined in the following spring and, with Veronica's help, the three produced *On Your Own in El Salvador,* OYO's first title. The book succeeded beyond their expectations and sold 10,000 in its first edition.

Out and About in Washington, DC represents a new twist in the publishing adventures of OYO. Its audience is the OYO traveler at home and at work or otherwise between trips to exotic destinations. Out and About answers the age-old question about what there is to do on a free afternoon or weekend besides a movie, video or a nap on the couch. With this book, the resident or frequent visitor to Washington, D.C. becomes an explorer of the region.

After a few adventures to the sites within this book, you will be able to say that, you've "been there, done that" around Washington DC. We are doing our best to write it all down and present it to you, the traveler, in a comprehensive, easy-to-read and entertaining format. We hope that you do your best to get up, get out and have some fun around our nation's capital.

As OYO explores more and more of the globe, throw us in your bag and we'll show you what the rest of the world is really about.

ss

Compact
Guide

Publisher Information

First published in Great Britain in 2000 by
Metropolis International (UK) Ltd.

ISBN 1 901811 38 7

COPYRIGHT

PUBLISHER

Metropolis International
222 Kensal Road
London W10 5BN
England

Telephone:
+44-(0)20-8964-4242

Fax:
+44-(0)20-8964-4141

E-mail:
admin@for-less.com

Web site:
www.for-less.com

US Office: Telephone:
+1-(212)-587-0287

Fax: +1-(212)-587-0247

DISCLAIMER

Assessments of attractions, hotels, museums and so
forth are based on the author's impressions and
therefore contain an element of subjective opinion
that may not reflect the opinion of the publishers.

The contents of this publication are believed to be
correct at the time of printing. However, details
such as opening times will change over time. We
would advise you to call ahead to confirm
important information.

All organizations offering discounts in this
guidebook have a contract with the publisher to
give genuine discounts to holders of valid *for less*
vouchers.

The publisher and/or its agents will not be
responsible if any establishment breaches its
contract (although it will attempt to secure
compliance) or if any establishment changes
ownership and the new owners refuse to honor the
contract.

Care has been taken to ensure that discounts are
only offered at reputable establishments, however,
the publisher and/or its agents cannot accept
responsibility for the quality of merchandise or
service provided, nor for errors or inaccuracies in
this guidebook.

The publisher will not be held responsible for any
loss, damage, injury, expense or inconvenience
sustained by any person, howsoever caused, as a
result of information or advice contained in this
guide except insofar as the law prevents the
exclusion of such liability.

ABBREVIATIONS

☎	Telephone Number
🕐	Opening times
Ⓜ	Nearest T station

Contents

HOW TO OBTAIN DISCOUNTS

Many of the museums and attractions in this guide offer discounts to holders of this book.

Museums and attractions which offer a discount are highlighted in pink in the text and designated by the following symbol in the margins:

To obtain your discount, simply hand in the appropriate voucher from the back of this book when you purchase your ticket.

Introduction to Boston

Autumn color at Harvard University

Boston is a living history lesson and a modern metropolis. You can travel through the centuries and look towards the future just by taking a short walk. It is a college town and an international city, a quaint seaport and a technological hotbed at the forefront of a burgeoning industry. It has the charming 19th-century townhouses of **Beacon Hill** (page 18) and the sweeping modern architecture of I.M. Pei's **JFK Library and Museum** (page 46). It is a city of contrasts that manages to succeed despite, or indeed because of, its polarity. Like the image of the Romanesque-style **Trinity Church** reflected in the sheer, glass facade of the **John Hancock Tower** (page 32), the distinction is sharp, yet somehow congruous.

The city's historic center, financial district and seat of government are all accessible by foot. For visitors, the heart of Boston is undoubtedly **Faneuil Hall** (page 10) and **Quincy Market** (page 11), in the area known as Government Center. From here, it is possible to visit the historic sites along the **Freedom Trail** (page 18), to explore the waterfront or to visit neighborhoods like the **North End** (page 24), Boston's "Little Italy".

Many of Boston's historic attractions offer interactive exhibits where you can relive history, or imagine life as it might have been. Throw chests of tea into the harbor, re-creating the famous "tea party", at the **Boston Tea Party Ship and Museum** (page 16), or see the home where **Paul Revere** lived when he set out for his historic ride (page 24). Stroll amidst the ivy-covered walls of **Harvard Yard** (page 39) in

Did you know...?

The Big Dig is the biggest and most complex highway project in American history. When it is finally completed in 2004, after more than a decade of grueling labor and engineering marvels, the freeway that now cuts off the waterfront and the North End from downtown Boston will be underground, leaving in its wake acres of parkland and modest new development. The project will also include the construction of a 14-lane, two-bridge crossing of the Charles River and the extension of the Massachusetts turnpike to Logan Airport, underneath the harbor. You can visit the website at www.bigdig.com to find out more.

Cambridge, where several buildings date to the early 18th century, or along nearby **Brattle Street** where the large number of royalists living here on the eve of the Revolution earned it the nick-name "Tory Row".

When you have had your fair share of history, you can enjoy a visit to the state-of-the-art **Museum of Science** and **Charles Hayden Planetarium** (page 23), the **Sports Museum of New England** at the new FleetCenter (page 22) or the **New England Aquarium** (page 15). You can also take advantage of Boston's many green spaces, take a cruise around the harbor or see a show in the theater district.

Music and art fans will enjoy Boston's rich cultural life. World-class museums like the **Museum of Fine Arts** (page 35) are supplemented by cutting-edge galleries, while fringe theatrical productions complement institutions like the **Boston Symphony**, **Boston Philharmonic** and the **Boston Ballet** (pages 54-55). For evening entertainment there are countless bars, clubs and music venues.

From ethnic eateries to starched fine-dining restaurants, Boston has a superb range of eating establishments. Traditional seafood is , and a visit here wouldn't be complete without trying chunky New England Clam Chowder soup, consumed with the requisite pint of locally-brewed ale. To sample two of Boston's specialties rolled into one, order up a seafood dish at one of the North End's lively Italian bistros.

Reflections

"A Boston man is the east wind made flesh"
– Thomas Gold Appleton

Reflections

"And this is good old Boston,
The home of the bean and the cod,
Where the Lowells talk to the Cabots
And the Cabots talk only to God" — John Collins Bossidy

IF YOU DO ONE THING . . .

1. If you visit one museum . . . the **Harvard Museum of Natural History** (page 40)

2. If you visit one church . . . **Trinity Church** (page 32)

3. If you go to one house museum . . . the **Paul Revere House** (page 24)

4. If you go to one room with a view . . . the **Observatory** at the **John Hancock Tower** (page 32)

5. If you visit one historic street . . . **Brattle Street**, Cambridge (page 41)

6. If you dine in one restaurant . . . **Legal Sea Foods** (page 50)

7. If you go to one art museum . . . the **Museum of Fine Arts** (page 35)

8. If you go to one shopping center . . . **Quincy Market** (page 52)

9. If you stroll in one park . . . the **Boston Public Garden** (page 29)

10. If you go on one excursion . . . **Lexington** (page 48)

History of Boston

By the time European explorers reached the area known today as **Massachusetts**, at the turn of the 16th century, mankind had already inhabited the region for almost 10,000 years. The Europeans called the area Massachusetts after the local Massachuset Indians.

Captain John Smith arrived in the Massachusetts Bay area in 1614 and, based on his reports, news of this "paradise" quickly spread throughout England. Escaping their home country to find religious freedom, a group of **Puritans** boarded the *Mayflower* in 1620, setting sail for the new world and establishing the first colony in **New England**. Although Boston itself wasn't actually founded until 1630, within two years it had become important enough to be named capital of the Massachusetts Bay Colony. By this time, the original Puritans, or "Pilgrims" as they came to be known, were already joined by enough English immigrants to swell the population.

By 1636, the development of Boston was well underway. An institute of higher education, **Harvard College**, was established in part to prepare young Puritans for the ministry. Society was stringently ruled by religion and the Puritans had little tolerance for any faith but their own. It was in this climate of paranoia and fanaticism that the notorious witch trials took place in Charleston, Boston and, most famously, Salem.

As the century progressed, the Puritans became more and more successful in manufacturing, commerce and trade, and Boston became one of the British Empire's largest and most important ports.

Did you know...?

The Massachusetts witch trials began under the strict Puritan climate of the 17th century. By the time the notorious Salem trials had ended in 1692, more than 200 people had been accused of practising witchcraft, 19 of them being hanged. Many others perished in captivity while awaiting trial. Over 500 original documents connected with the trials can be seen at the **Peabody Essex Museum** (page 49).

An early map of Massachusetts and the surrounding states

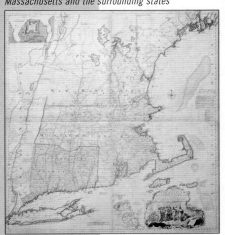

Boston Tea Party Ship and Museum

The French and Indian Wars of 1754-1763 left the Empire with a debt that it expected the colonists to help pay. Outraged by the tariffs imposed on goods ranging from newspapers to tea, the colonists staged boycotts and protests. As time passed, the advantages of separation became more and more obvious, and future Revolutionary leaders like **Samuel Adams** began to speak out on the issue.

In 1768, **King George III** sent troops to Boston to keep the peace, yet the occupation only caused tensions to mount. When British soldiers killed five colonists in a skirmish in front of the **Old State House**, news of the "Boston Massacre" traveled swiftly and gave anti-royalists a new point on which to converge.

In a repentant move, the king revoked many of the taxes imposed by the **Townshend Acts** of 1767, except that on the most popular beverage in the colony – tea. Colonists replied by boycotting imported tea, and British ships which had already reached the harbor were left with no-one to buy their cargo. They refused to leave until the tea was taken, but even after the tax was finally revoked, the colonist merchants refused to buy. In December 1773, a group of colonists calling themselves the "**Sons of Liberty**" boarded the ships and threw 342 chests of tea overboard in the most defiant act yet committed by the colonists. This event

Did you know...?

Boston's first major industry was shipping. The clipper ships produced by early Boston shipbuilders were considered among the best in the world. Boston's seaport still thrives, even if today's ships depart full of tourists instead of silks and tea.

Faneuil Hall

Did you know...?

The patriot Minutemen soldiers were so-called because they took just one minute to be dressed and ready to fight when called to action.

became known as the **Boston Tea Party**.

Each side increasingly distrusted the other, and soon the British took steps to confiscate the arms and ammunition accumulated by the patriots. On April 18th, 1775, British troops set out for nearby Concord, while **Paul Revere**, **William Dawes** and **Samuel Prescott** set out to warn the patriots of their approach. The British Redcoats got as far as **Lexington** before the patriot **Minutemen** surprised them with a scuffle on Lexington Green. But the troops marched on unchecked until the first, and only, real battle of the American Revolution fought on Massachusetts soil, at **Breed's Hill**. Mistakenly reported as having taken place on nearby **Bunker Hill**, the battle was won by the British, but at a severe price. Reports suggest that the British lost nearly half their troops. The patriots had proved themselves to be a worthy foe and their bravery galvanized freedom-fighters throughout the colonies.

The breakdown of relations with Britain following the Revolution hurt Boston's trade, but its shipping industry soon found alternative markets and, when its famous clipper ships were eventually replaced by the new steamships, manufacturing boomed.

Jobs in the new industries, as in other American cities, were filled by newly arriving immigrants. The potato famine brought huge numbers of **Irish** immigrants. They were followed by other ethnic groups, who comprised more than half the population by the mid-19th century. The population explosion was matched by physical growth that included the creation of new neighbourhoods, such as **Back Bay** and **South End**.

Boston's merchant class, known as the

"**Boston Brahmins**", grew very rich. Through their travels abroad, they came to desire the art and culture of the European cities. Museums, theaters and other cultural institutions were created, literature flourished and Boston earned itself the nickname the "**Athens of America**".

Boston was also more progressive than much of the country on the issue of slavery. Massachusetts had abolished slavery in 1783 and blacks were allowed to worship freely and educate themselves, even though they did not yet have the right to vote. In 1832, the **New England Anti-Slavery Society** was formed. Blacks and whites alike spoke out for Abolition, and when the Civil War broke out in 1863, one of the society's members, **Frederick Douglass**, helped organize the 54th and 55th Massachusetts Colored Regiments whose tale was told in the film *Glory*.

The 20th century saw the rise of new industries, a burgeoning population and the World Wars that depressed and bolstered the economy in turn. Middle- and upper-class Bostonians fled to the suburbs in droves, a phenomenon which came to be called "white flight". The immigrant success story unfolded as Irish-Catholic Bostonians saw one of their own, **John F. Kennedy**, become President of the United States.

Academia in Boston flourished as new colleges and universities were founded and established ones such as Harvard and the MIT expanded. In the 1960s and 1970s, they became political hotbeds for issues such as Vietnam, desegregation of schools and civil rights.

At the start of the 21st century, Boston continues to enjoy an international reputation for higher learning, and to play a major role in the development of new technologies.

Don't miss...

For a unique historical perspective, step back in time at one of Boston's colonial cemeteries. One of the country's oldest is the **Old Granary Burying Ground** (page 22), with its elaborately carved gravestones and solemn ambience. Here you can visit the final resting place of many of Boston's best-known figures, including Paul Revere, Samuel Adams and John Hancock.

Paul Revere

Downtown Boston

City Hall

Congress Street
Ⓜ Government Center

Faneuil Hall and Quincy Market

Congress Street
between State and
North Streets
Ⓜ Government Center,
State Street or
Haymarket
☎ 338-2323
🕓 Faneuil Hall and
Museum: Mon-Sun: 9am-
5pm. Informational
talks every 20 minutes.
🕓 Marketplace: Mon-
Sat: 10am-9pm. Sun:
12noon-6pm.
Restaurants open later.
Admission free.

Union Oyster House

41 Union Street
Ⓜ Government Center,
State Street or
Haymarket
☎ 227-2750
🕓 Sun-Thu: 11am-
9.30pm. Fri-Sat: 11am-
10pm. Bar open later.

In this guidebook, the area known as Downtown Boston includes Government Center, the Financial District, the waterfront wharves and Chinatown. Boston's compact size means that most areas are easily accessible by foot, and by following the two and a half mile (4km) Freedom Trail (see page 18), you can trace the history of Boston dating from colonial times. Most of the historic sites along the trail are situated within this area and are described in detail below.

The heart of Government Center is **City Hall**, a modern complex that serves as the seat of city government. Built in the 1960s, this modern complex, with its stark, brick plaza, is seen as an architectural achievement to some and a bleak monstrosity to others. Either way, it stands in sharp contrast to historic Faneuil Hall, located just across the street.

Also in City Hall Plaza, near Sudbury Street, the twin towers which comprise the **John F. Kennedy Federal Office Building** were designed by Walter Gropius, founder of the Bauhaus architectural movement. To see more of his work, you can visit his personal home, Gropius House (page 48), in nearby Lincoln.

Faneuil Hall was built as a meeting place and market for the town in 1742, a gift from merchant Peter Faneuil. The building's Great Hall hosted many public speakers in the years leading up to the Revolution and became known as the "Cradle of Liberty" for the part it played in igniting the war. In the years to follow, it would continue to play an important role in the many causes and movements affecting the nation, including slavery and civil rights.

The hall is open to the public when not in use for special functions, meetings or the occasional concert. The fourth floor is occupied by an exhibit of artillery artifacts belonging to the museum of the **Ancient and Honorable Artillery Company of Massachusetts**, the oldest military company in the U.S., dating to 1638.

Faneuil Hall and its markets are Boston's

top draw for tourists, receiving more than 13 million visitors per year, and they make a great starting place for a tour of historical Boston. For first-time visitors, there may be some confusion about the complex since it is referred to by a variety of names. Faneuil Hall, itself containing several shops, is adjacent to **Quincy Market**, so the market is also sometimes called Faneuil Hall Marketplace. In addition, although Quincy Market is the name of the central market building, flanked by the **North**

Quincy Market

and **South Market** buildings, the name is often used to refer to the whole complex. However you refer to it, the markets contain over 150 shops and restaurants and make up the bustling hub of central Boston (see also *Shopping*, pages 52-53).

Claiming to be the country's oldest restaurant in continuous operation, the **Union Oyster House** opened in 1826. Famous guests, such as Daniel Webster and President John F. Kennedy, whose favorite booth is designated with a plaque, have enjoyed the hearty traditional American fare. Not surprisingly, seafood figures prominently on the menu, and the original Oyster Bar is as famous as the restaurant itself.

Across the street from the restaurant, the steel and glass structure of the **New England Holocaust Memorial** stands in sharp contrast to its centuries-old neighbors. The dramatic design was chosen from an international competition and erected in 1995.

In the shadow of the looming Fitzgerald Expressway, **Haymarket** (see also *Shopping*, pages 52-53) is an open-air market peddling seafood, fruits, vegetables and more.

Following the steps of the Freedom Trail

New England Holocaust Memorial

Congress and Union Streets
Ⓜ Government Center, State Street or Haymarket

Haymarket

Marshall and Blackstone Streets
Ⓜ Haymarket
🕐 Fri-Sat: 7am-2pm.

King's Chapel / King's Chapel Burying Ground

58 Tremont Street
Ⓜ Park Street,
Government Center
☎ 227-2155
🕐 May-Aug: Mon and
Fri-Sat: 10am-4pm. Tue-
Thu and Sun: closed.
Sep-Apr: Sat: 10am-4pm.
Sun-Fri: closed.
Admission free.

Old City Hall

41-45 School Street
Ⓜ State Street/
Government Center

Old Corner Bookstore

1 School Street
Ⓜ State Street/
Downtown Crossing
☎ 367-4000
🕐 Mon-Fri: 9am-
5.30pm. Sat: 9.30am-
5pm. Sun: 11am-4pm.
Admission free.

out of Boston Common and past the Granary Burying Ground (page 22), you will encounter the **King's Chapel** and the adjacent **King's Chapel Burying Ground** on the corner of Tremont and School Streets. The King's Chapel was the first Anglican church in Boston, though not surprisingly, it was converted after the Revolution and became the country's first Unitarian church. The granite building that you see was completed in 1754, constructed *around* the original wooden structure, itself dating to 1688, which was taken down when the new shell was complete. You will undoubtedly notice that the top of the building appears to be cut off abruptly. The steeple, originally planned in the design, was not completed due to a lack of funds.

Adjacent to the church, the Burying Ground is Boston's oldest, dating to 1630, and contains the remains of many famous Bostonians. Check the map at the entrance to find the graves of John Winthrop, the first governor of Massachusetts, John Dawes, who rode with Paul Revere to Lexington and Concord (see page 25), Elizabeth Pain, after whom the character Hester Prynne was based in Nathaniel Hawthorne's *The Scarlet Letter*, and Mary Chilton, the first woman to disembark from the *Mayflower* in Plymouth.

Around the corner, on School Street, the elegant **Old City Hall** dates to 1865. The city government remained in this building until the opening of Government Center in 1969. Today, offices and a restaurant occupy the site. The statue of Benjamin Franklin in front is significant for being the first portrait statue erected in the country. On the sidewalk in front of the Old City Hall, a plaque marks the site of the **First Public School**, the Boston Latin School, established in 1635. Among the students who attended the school were John Hancock, Samuel Adams and Benjamin Franklin.

Further along School Street is the site of the **Old Corner Bookstore**, marked by a plaque on the building's façade. Originally built as an apothecary shop and residence, the building dates to 1718 and belonged to the Ticknor and Fields Publishing House from 1832 to 1865. During its heyday, it was the center of the literary world, catering to customers like Charles Dickens, Henry David Thoreau, Ralph Waldo Emerson and Harriet Beecher Stowe. The literary tradition continues today with the present occupant, the Boston Globe Store.

In the small square in front of the Old Corner Bookstore, you will notice the two sculptures that comprise the **Memorial to the Irish Famine**. Portraying the pain and struggle of the old country and the hope of the new, the memorial is a tribute to the many Irish immigrants who came to live in Boston. It was erected in 1998, on the 150th anniversary of the Irish Potato Famine. (School and Washington Streets, Ⓜ State Street.)

Across the street, the **Old South Meeting House** proudly dominates the square. When it was built in 1729, the meeting house was the largest building in Boston. It served as an important place for colonists to voice their outrage at what they felt were injustices put upon them under British rule. One key protest took place in 1773, when over 5,000 colonists descended upon the meeting house infuriated about the tea tax, thus sparking the famous Boston Tea Party. This story is presented in an audio program available at the site.

Just around the corner, on Milk Street, is the site of **Benjamin Franklin's Birthplace**. The original house where he was born in

Old South Meeting House

310 Washington Street
Ⓜ State Street
☎ 482-6439
🕐 Mon-Sun:
9.30am-5pm.
Admission charge.

New England Telephone Building

185 Franklin Street
Ⓜ State Street/
Downtown Crossing
☎ 743-4886
🕐 Mon-Fri: 8.30am-
5pm. Sat-Sun: closed.
Admission free.

Old Corner Bookstore

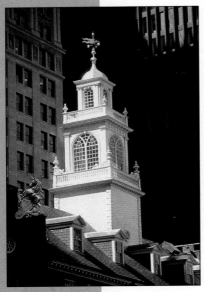

Old State House

1706 no longer exists, but the 19th-century building which stands on the site today has the words "Birthplace of Benjamin Franklin" carved into its façade. *(17 Milk Street, Ⓜ State Street.)*

The **New England Telephone Building** would be a rather ordinary office building if not for an interesting exhibition in its lobby. In 1875, Alexander Graham Bell first transmitted his voice by telephone. The structure in which this historic event took place was demolished in the 1920s, but the phone company took the opportunity to transport the room, piece by piece, so that today you can visit Bell's workshop and see how it would have looked at the time of his invention.

The **Old State House** is the oldest public building in Boston, dating from 1713. Before the Revolution it was the seat of the colonial British government and after it was the seat of the new Commonwealth of Massachusetts until the new State House was built on Beacon Street (page 19). The Declaration of Independence was read for the first time in public on July 18th, 1776 from the east balcony. The event is recreated in commemoration every July 4th.

Below the east balcony is a memorial to those killed by British soldiers in what became known as the Boston Massacre of 1770. The **Site of the Boston Massacre** is marked by a circle of cobblestones which today lies on a traffic island in front of the Old State House.

The **Boston Athenaeum** is one of the most revered exhibition spaces in Boston. The Athenaeum library collection, named for Boston's reputation as the "Athens of America", existed for some forty years before moving to this location in 1849. Today it remains a private organization

Old State House

206 Washington Street
Ⓜ State Street
☎ 720-3290
🕐 Mon-Sun: 9am-5pm.
Admission charge.

Boston Athenaeum

10½ Beacon Street
Ⓜ Park Street
☎ 227-0270
🕐 Under renovation until 2001. Call ahead for hours and details of free tours.

whose members can relax with a good book in one of the many finely decorated reading rooms. The library is under renovation until at least 2001, so call ahead to find out details about hours and tours.

When the **U.S. Customs House** was built in 1847, it lacked the tower that you see today and its location was actually on the harbor. The addition of the tower in 1915 gained the building the title of Boston's tallest, and today it is several streets inland. The U.S. government sold the building in 1987, and today the building is used for plush timeshare apartments.

Across the expressway, behind Haymarket, lies a group of attractions along the waterfront. **Long Wharf** was originally known as Boston Pier when it became a hub of trading during the 18th century. At the foot of the wharf, **Columbus Park** is a quiet stretch of green dividing this area from the North End (pages 24-27). The park is a favorite destination for tourists who dine at one of the many restaurants on the waterfront or in the North End. (Atlantic Avenue, at Commercial Wharf and Long Wharf.)

From the wharf, you can pick up harbor tours and visit the **Boston Harbor Islands State Park**. The harbor islands number more than thirty and count among them several historic sites. You can reach the islands by water taxi or by taking the ferry.

One of Boston's finest attractions and a favorite with families, the **New England Aquarium** is situated on Central Wharf, at the foot of Milk Street. With over 20,000 species of marine wildlife on display, the aquarium boasts one of the largest aquatic collections in the world. The centerpiece of the museum is the incredible 200,000-gallon Giant Ocean Tank. Inside, you can see sharks, giant sea turtles, sting rays and countless varieties of tropical fish. If you are there at feeding time, you can watch the divers descend into the three-story tank and feed the many sea creatures.

Interactive exhibits allow you to gain a deeper understanding of the life of a marine mammal. Other things to look for are the sea lions, otters and penguins. The

---

U.S. Customs House

3 McKinley Square
Ⓜ Aquarium
🕐 Not open to the public.

Boston Harbor Islands State Park

Boats leave from Long Wharf
Ⓜ Aquarium
☎ 727-7676
🕐 Jun-Sep: call ahead for schedule and transportation information.

New England Aquarium

Central Wharf
Ⓜ Aquarium
☎ 973-5200
www.neaq.org
🕐 Jul-Aug: Mon-Tue & Fri: 9am-6pm. Wed-Thu: 9am-8pm. Sat-Sun & holidays: 9am-7pm. Sep-Jun: Mon-Fri: 9am-5pm. Sat-Sun & holidays: 9am-6pm.
Admission charge.
2 admissions for the price of 1 with voucher on page 63.

"tidepool" gives you a first-hand look at the environment that is home to starfish, hermit crabs, sea urchins and more.

Also located at the Aquarium, the interactive film experience **Unforgettable Boston** captures the unique flavor of the city, while allowing visitors to guide the story by touching private console screens. The audience can choose the locations where the story unfolds and get information on hundreds of Boston's attractions and events.

The promenade of **Rowes Wharf** is one of the most elegant and pleasant places to take in the harbor and the pristine yachts docked in the marina. It would be hard to imagine a better spot to arrive in Boston than here. If you fly into Logan Airport, this is where you will be when the water shuttle drops you off.

The **Boston Tea Party Ship and Museum** allows you to participate in the rebellious act of throwing chests of tea overboard from the *Beaver II*, an authentic replica of one of the British ships moored in the harbor during the famous "tea party". The exhibition center provides more information about the event and its important role in the Revolution through audio and video displays, illustrations and lively text. The complimentary tea is an added touch that pleasantly reinforces the theme.

The **Children's Museum of Boston** is a place where children can have fun while learning by exploring, experimenting and discovering. The second-oldest such museum in the world, it is also one of the largest. Four floors are packed with hands-on exhibits, a participatory theater and even a special area just for infants and toddlers.

Kids can do everything from blow bubbles to climb a two-story maze to play dress up. They can "truck" into the Construction Zone or steer their own boat through a mini Boston Harbor. A popular spot is Arthur's™ World, based on the PBS television show and book series. There is a 170-year-old Japanese house to explore, and a child-sized grocery store in which to shop.

The museum's waterfront location also

Unforgettable Boston

Central Wharf
Ⓜ Aquarium
☎ (800) 296-7600
🕐 Call ahead for schedule.
Admission charge.
2 admissions for the price of 1 with voucher on page 63.

Boston Tea Party Ship and Museum

300 Congress Street Bridge
Ⓜ South Station
☎ 338-1773
www.historictours.com
🕐 Jun-Aug: Mon-Sun: 9am-6pm. Sep-Nov & Mar-May: Mon-Sun: 9am-5pm. Dec-Feb & Thanksgiving: closed.
Admission charge.
2 admissions for the price of 1 with voucher on page 63.

makes it an especially pleasant place for a summer picnic. To fully enjoy the museum, it is recommended that you allow one and a half to three hours for your visit, though many visitors stay longer.

A transportation hub, the grand **South Station** is the terminus for Amtrak trains, the location of a T station and is across the street from the South Station Transportation Center, also known simply as the bus depot. Unless you travel by air, it is likely that you will pass through the station in your travels. *(Atlantic Avenue and Summer Street.)*

The **Leather District**, across from South Station between Atlantic Avenue and Kneeland Street, was the bustling center of the leather trade, one that flourished towards the end of the 19th century. Today, the historic buildings are more likely to house an art gallery or trendy boutique than a garment shop, but the newly gentrified area is much loved and has earned a reputation as the "Soho" of Boston. *(Roughly bounded by Kneeland, Lincoln and Atlantic, Ⓜ South Station.)*

Bordering the Leather District is **Chinatown**, home to a huge Asian population which includes not only Chinese, but also Korean, Vietnamese, Cambodian and other nationalities. The formal entranceway into the area is the three-story **Chinatown Gateway** at Beach Street, the area's main thoroughfare, just west of the Leather District. Even if you didn't enter here, it would be hard not to recognize the profusion of signs marked by Chinese characters and realize where you are. Chinatown draws Bostonians from all over the city for celebrations during the Chinese New Year, and anytime when seeking a quality Asian meal at a fair price (see *Dining*, pages 50-51).

Children's Museum of Boston

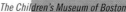

300 Congress Street
Ⓜ South Station
☎ 426-8855
www.bostonkids.org
⏰ Mon-Sun: 10am-5pm (9pm Fri). Closed Thanksgiving & Christmas Day. Admission charge.
2 admissions for the price of 1 with voucher on page 63.

The Children's Museum of Boston

Boston Common, Beacon Hill and the West End

Boston Common

Walking through the historic streets of **Beacon Hill**, visitors could be forgiven for craning their necks to catch a peek of an interior through the closing door of an enchanting townhouse. The good news is that several of these historic homes are open to the public, including the Harrison Gray Otis House (page 21), Prescott House (page 19) and Nichols House Museum (page 20).

The fact that nearly all of the houses on Beacon Hill were constructed in the first half of the 19th century creates a consistency of style and the feeling of having been transported back to another time. Brick is everywhere, from the facades of the Federal-style buildings to the sidewalks which, by law, must stay that way. Several organizations, such as the Beacon Hill Architectural Commission, have long ensured that the historical integrity of the neighborhood remains. Stringent regulation of exterior design and alteration applies, right down to the color of the doors.

Freedom Trail

Information kiosk
Tremont Street

While the south side of the slope had long been a bastion of Boston's elite, the north side was inhabited by a community of free blacks who settled in around the beginning of the 19th century. Several sites that mark the role they played in the anti-slavery movement and their importance in this country's history are included in the Black Heritage Trail (page 21), a walking tour based on the concept of the Freedom Trail (below).

Beacon Street

A good place to begin a tour of Beacon Hill is with the picturesque **Boston Common**, the oldest public park in the country, created in 1634. The 50-acre (20-hectare) park has always served as a public gathering place and has been the backdrop for events ranging from public hangings to rallies and protests to baseball games. The park is dotted with statues and monuments, a bandstand, an early burying ground and a frog pond, which is transformed into a popular ice skating rink during the cold winter months.

American Meteorology Society

45 Beacon Street
🕐 No admission to the public.

Boston Common is also the place to embark on the **Freedom Trail**, starting at the

Beacon Street

information kiosk on the Tremont Street side of the park. Pick up the free map and guide at the kiosk and follow the red dotted line which traces the path of the early patriots on their journey to freedom. The two and a half-mile (4km) walking trail wends through downtown Boston, the North End and into Charlestown, passing sixteen of Boston's historic sites along the way.

Running along the north side of the park is stately **Beacon Street**. It is the prestigious address for some of the grandest mansions in a neighborhood known for its grand mansions. Many of these early 19th-century homes were designed by the renowned architect Charles Bulfinch, including the most palatial of the three **Harrison Gray Otis** houses (see also page 21) at number 45, where the ultra-wealthy Mr. Otis lived for over 40 years. Today, the house is used as the headquarters for the **American Meteorology Society**.

A few doors down, at number 55, the Federal-style **Prescott House** was once the home of historian William Hickling Prescott. Designed by Asher Benjamin in 1808, it is today open to the public as a museum. In addition to showcasing a fine interior and period antiques, it also displays a unique collection of costumes.

Dividing Boston Common from the Boston Public Garden (page 29), **Charles Street** runs down the middle of the two green spaces and continues into Beacon Hill, becoming the area's main commercial thoroughfare. Rife with antique and

Prescott House

55 Beacon Street
Ⓜ Park Street/Arlington
☎ 742-3190
🕐 Mid May-Oct: Wed-Thu and Sat: 12noon-4pm. Fri and Sun-Tue: closed. Nov-mid May: closed.
Admission charge.
2 admissions for the price of 1 with voucher on page 63.

Charles Street

Nichols House Museum

55 Mount Vernon Street
Ⓜ Park Street/Charles Street
☎ 227-6993
🕐 May-Oct: Tue-Sat: 12.15pm-4.15pm. Sun-Mon: closed. Nov-Dec and Feb-Apr: Thu-Sat: 12.15pm-4.15pm. Sun-Wed: closed. Jan: closed. Admission charge.
2 admissions for the price of 1 with voucher on page 63.

Louisberg Square

Acorn Street

artisan's shops, Charles Street manages to evoke the feeling of a village or intimate neighborhood of another time. The delicate scale of the buildings, brick walkways and gas lamps certainly add to the atmosphere.

Running off Charles Street, you will find two of the most prestigious residential streets in Beacon Hill – **Chestnut Street** and **Mount Vernon Street**. From the day houses were first built here, the addresses have spoken for themselves. Among Boston's prominent residents who have made their home here are Henry James *(131 Mount Vernon Street)*, Robert Frost *(88 Mount Vernon Street)* and Henry Kissinger *(1 Chestnut Street)*.

For a taste of life on one of these streets, step through the front door of the dignified four-story townhouse which today functions as the **Nichols House Museum**. The house was constructed in 1804 in the Federal style from a design attributed to celebrated architect Charles Bulfinch (see page 19).

Evidence of updates and evolving architectural styles are reflected throughout, from the Greek Revival entryway added to the exterior to the lighting fixtures which began as candle and oil lamps but have more recently been modernized with electricity. European and Asian art, oriental rugs, ancestral portraits and other Nichols family possessions furnish the house. The museum was established in 1961 through a legacy of the late Rose Standish Nichols, the last family member to occupy the home.

Just off Mount Vernon Street, the grandeur continues with the only example of a planned square on Beacon Hill. The houses around dignified **Louisberg Square** are elegance and wealth defined. Meticulously maintained, they face onto a private green, surrounded by a black wrought-iron fence. Among the most famous residents of the square was Louisa May Alcott who lived at number 10.

On the other side of Mount Vernon Street, between Willow and Cedar, is **Acorn Street**, undoubtedly one of the most picturesque and most photographed streets in Boston. Less grand than the streets mentioned above, Acorn is lined with quaint brick homes once belonging to humble craftsmen and artisans.

On Cambridge Street, the **Harrison Gray Otis House** was the first of the three houses built by Charles Bulfinch for prominent lawyer, politician and real estate developer Harrison Gray Otis. The house, built in 1796, is a fine example of the elegant proportions and delicate detail typical of the Federal style. The restoration of this home, with its brightly colored carpeting and fine furniture, is historically accurate down to the smallest details.

Nearby, on Smith Street, lies one of the most important stops along the **Black Heritage Trail** – the **Museum of African-American History**. The museum encompasses the **Abiel Smith School** (46 Joy Street) which opened in 1834 as a grammar school for black students and the **African Meeting House**, the oldest black church building in the U.S. The 1806 building was mainly constructed by African-Americans and functioned as the area's hub. It was known as the "black Faneuil Hall" for the critical role it played in rallying the community, especially on the subject of slavery. It was here that the New England Anti-Slavery Society was founded in 1832, led by William Lloyd Garrison and supported by blacks and whites alike.

At the top of Park Street, on Beacon Street, stands Charles Bulfinch's most ambitious and famous project, the **Massachusetts State House**. Dating from 1795, this gold-domed building is the oldest on Beacon Hill, and is widely regarded as one of the finest public buildings in the country. The cornerstone was laid by Governor Samuel Adams, and the copper sheathing on the dome was

Harrison Gray Otis House

141 Cambridge Street, entrance on Lynde Street
Ⓜ Bowdoin/Charles St.
☎ 227-3956
www.spnea.org
Wed-Sun: 11am-5pm. Mon-Tue: closed. Last tour at 4pm.
Admission charge.
2 admissions for the price of 1 with voucher on page 63.

Museum of African-American History

8 Smith Court
Ⓜ Park Street
☎ 725-0022
Jun-Aug: Mon-Sun: 10am-4pm. Sep-May: Mon-Sat: 10am-4pm. Sun: closed.
Donation suggested.

Massachusetts State House

Beacon Street
Ⓜ Park Street
☎ 727-3676
Mon-Sat: 10am-3.30pm. Tours every ½ hour. Tours are free, but reservations are recommended.

Park Street Church

0-3 Park Street
Ⓜ Park Street
☎ 523-3383
🕐 Tours: Mid-Jun-Aug:
Tue-Sat: 9.30am-3.30pm.
Services: Sun: 8.30am,
11am, 4.30pm and 7pm.

**FleetCenter
(Sports Museum)**

1 Causeway Street
Ⓜ North Station
☎ 624-1000
www.fleetcenter.com
Museum: Premium
Seating Levels 5 & 6:
☎ 624-1234
🕐 Tue-Sat: 10am-5pm.
Sun: 12noon-5pm.
Mon: closed (hours
subject to change due to
FleetCenter events).
Admission charge.
**2 admissions for the
price of 1 with voucher
on page 65.**

**Massachusetts General
Hospital**

55 Fruit Street
Ⓜ Charles/MGH
☎ 726-2000
Etherdome:
☎ 726-2397
🕐 Mon-Sun: 9am-5pm.
Admission free.

supplied by Paul Revere's foundry. It continues to serve as the seat of government for the Commonwealth of Massachusetts. Inside, visitors can examine the House and Senate Chambers and see the Hall of Flags on the free 45-minute tours.

At the opposite end of Park Street, at the corner of Tremont Street, the 1810 Congregationalist **Park Street Church** is recognizable by its tall, white steeple. In 1829, this was the location of William Lloyd Garrison's first abolitionist speech. Two years later, "America the Beautiful" made its debut here.

Next to the church, on Tremont Street, the **Old Granary Burying Ground** dates to 1660 and is one of the country's oldest and most hauntingly beautiful, no pun intended. The gravestones are marked with carvings of skulls, skeletons, angels and more pairs of wings than you can count. Some of Boston's most famous denizens are buried here, including Samuel Adams, Paul Revere, John Hancock, the parents of Ben Franklin and Mother Goose, of nursery rhyme fame. *(Tremont Street,* Ⓜ *Park Street,* ☎ *635-4505.* 🕐 *Mon-Sun: dawn to dusk. Admission free.)*

North of Beacon Hill lies an area known as the **West End**. Once a warren of narrow streets and crumbling tenements, a 1960s urban-planning project cleared most of the area and rebuilt it. Many believe the plan backfired, displacing hundreds of low-income families from this shabby but affordable enclave, leaving in its wake a slew of cold, modern high-rises.

One of the biggest projects to come out of the reconstruction was the **FleetCenter**, which replaced the Boston Garden. Home to the Celtics basketball team and Bruins hockey team, the arena also hosts entertainment events such as concerts and ice shows.

Located on the fifth and sixth floors of the FleetCenter is the **Sports Museum of New England**. A great place for sports fans of all ages, the museum features hockey, football, soccer, baseball, boxing, and many other sports through artwork,

Massachusetts State House

memorabilia, interactive exhibits and multimedia. You can learn about the sporting traditions of New England's professional, collegiate, Olympic and high school teams and athletes.

Massachusetts General Hospital, founded in 1811, is one of the most renowned general hospitals in the country. The 1818 Bulfinch Pavilion is the work of architect Charles Bulfinch. The hospital is most famous, however, for Dr. John Collins Warren's 1846 surgical breakthrough of anesthetizing patients with ether. You can visit the Etherdome where this event took place and see a display about its historical importance.

Straddling the Charles River, between Boston and Cambridge, the **Museum of Science** is one of Boston's premier museums and a favorite destination for anyone visiting Boston. There are more than 600 interactive exhibits, with topics ranging from electricity and optical illusions to physics and light. Don't miss the Virtual Fishtank and Cahners ComputerPlace, two exciting new additions.

The **Charles Hayden Planetarium** boasts a state-of-the-art multimedia system which is used for astronomy and laser light shows.

A separate admission charge also applies for shows on Boston's largest movie screen at the adjacent **Mugar Omni Theater** (☎ 723-2500).

Museum of Science

Science Park
Ⓜ Science Park
☎ 723-2500
www.mos.org
🕐 Jul-mid-Sep: Sat-Thu: 9am-7pm. Fri: 9am-9pm. Mid-Sep-Jul: Mon-Sun: 9am-5pm. Admission charge.

for less **Charles Hayden Planetarium**

Science Park
Ⓜ Science Park
☎ 523-6664
www.mos.org
🕐 Labor Day-Jul 4: Sat-Thu: 9am-5pm. Fri: 9am-9pm. Jul 5-Labor Day: Sat-Thu: 9am-7pm. Fri: 9am-9pm. Admission charge.
2 admissions for the price of 1 with voucher on page 65.

The North End and Charlestown

Paul Revere House

19 North Square
Ⓜ Haymarket/Aquarium
☎ 523-2338
www.paulreverehouse.org
🕘 Nov-mid-Apr: Mon-
Sun: 9.30am-4.15pm.
Mid-Apr-Oct: Mon-Sun:
9.30am-5.15pm. Jan-
Mar: Mon: closed.
Admission charge.
**2 admissions for the
price of 1 with voucher
on page 65.**

The **North End** is the historical heart of Boston, and its narrow, winding streets reveal its origins as a colonial outpost. In the 17th and early 18th centuries, the North End *was* Boston, as areas like Beacon Hill and Back Bay did not yet exist. From about 1820 onward, the neighborhood received a steady flow of immigrants of many nationalities, including African-Americans, Irish, Eastern European Jews, Portuguese and, finally, Italians.

For the last 60 years or so, the North End has come to be known as Boston's "Little Italy". Scores of Italian restaurants and cafés line **Hanover Street** and **Salem Street**, the neighborhood's two main thoroughfares. Both locals and tourists alike flock here in droves for a good Italian meal, followed by pastries and an espresso or cappuccino (see *Dining*, pages 50-51).

The North End is also of historical importance in a specific sense. It is the location of Paul Revere's house (below) from where he set out to warn patriots in Lexington about the onward-marching British troops. His journey took him across the Charles River and through **Charlestown**, where today there are several attractions of note.

The c.1680 **Paul Revere House** is downtown Boston's oldest and most famous residence, and the only house located along the Freedom Trail (page 18). Revere was living in this house when, on the eve of the Revolution in 1775, he, William Dawes and Samuel Prescott embarked on the famous journey

Paul Revere House

by land and water to Lexington to warn patriot leaders Samuel Adams and John Hancock that the British troops were *en route* to arrest them and seize their hidden munitions.

Originally built after a fire swept the North End in 1676, destroying forty structures, the house first belonged to wealthy merchant Robert Howard. Almost a hundred years later, after many alterations and updates, Paul Revere bought the house in 1770 and owned it until 1800. It was later divided into tenements to house the many immigrants that flooded the area, and at various times also served as a grocery store, bank and even a cigar factory.

In 1902, Paul Revere's great-grandson, John P. Reynolds, Jr., stepped in and saved the house from impending demolition. It has since been restored to reflect the 17th-century lifestyle of its original owner, as well as that of its most famous residents, Paul Revere and his family.

Adjacent to the Paul Revere House, the **Pierce/Hichborn House** is one of only a few remaining examples of early 18th-century brick architecture. Built around 1711, the house embodied many of the architectural features of the Georgian style, new at the time. Originally owned by Moses Pierce, a glazier by trade, it was later occupied by Nathaniel Hichborn, a boat builder and first cousin to Paul Revere. The Pierce/Hichborn House is shown by guided tour only, so call ahead for details.

St. Stephen's Church, built in 1804, has the distinction of being the only church remaining in Boston designed by the city's most renowned architect, Charles Bulfinch. Originally Unitarian, the church became Roman Catholic in 1862. It also has ties to one of the most famous Catholic families in America – the Kennedys. The baptism of the future Rose Fitzgerald Kennedy, matriarch of the clan, was held here, as was her funeral 104 years later.

Before Paul Revere's famous "ride" to

Pierce/Hichborn House

29 North Square
Ⓜ Haymarket/Aquarium
☎ 523-2338
🕐 Nov-mid-Apr: Mon-Sun: 9.30am-4.15pm.
Mid-Apr-Oct: Mon-Sun: 9.30am-5.15pm. Jan-Mar: Mon: closed. Tours usually given at 12.30pm and 2.30pm, but the schedule varies seasonally, so call ahead.
Charge for tours.

St. Stephen's Church

24 Clark Street
Ⓜ Haymarket/Aquarium
☎ 523-1230
🕐 Mon-Sun: 9am-5pm.
Sun: mass at 8.30am & 11am.
Admission free.

Old North Church

193 Salem Street
Ⓜ Haymarket/Aquarium
☎ 523-6676
🕐 Mon-Sun: 9am-5pm.
Services on Sundays at 9am, 11am & 5pm.
Admission free.

USS Constitution

Copp's Hill Burying Ground

Hull Street at Snowhill
Ⓜ North Station
🕐 Mon-Sun: dawn to dusk.
Admission free.

USS *Constitution*

Charlestown Navy Yard
☎ 242-5670
🕐 Free guided tours:
Mon-Sun: 9.30am-3.50pm.
Museum:
Constitution Wharf
☎ 426-1812
🕐 Nov-Apr: Mon-Sun:
10am-5pm. May-Oct:
Mon-Sun: 9am-6pm.
Admission free.

Lexington on April 18th, 1775 (page 24), he went first to Christ Church, now known as the **Old North Church**, and instructed the sexton, Robert Newman, to hang two lanterns in the steeple. Visible from the Charlestown shore, this signal was prearranged to inform patriots there that the British troops were coming.

Situated between the two landmark churches mentioned above is **Paul Revere Mall**, also known as the Prado. Lining the mall are brick walls marked by bronze plaques recounting the stories of famous North End residents. The centerpiece of the mall is the equestrian statue of Paul Revere, designed in 1865, but not erected until 1940. *(Between Unity Street and Hanover Street.)*

Several blocks away, on Hull Street, the **Copp's Hill Burying Ground** is the final stop on the Freedom Trail before leaving the North End. Situated on land given to the town by the Copp family, this cemetery dates to 1659 and is one of the oldest in Boston. It is the final resting place for over 10,000 Bostonians including Robert Newman (see above), Puritan religious leader Cotton Mather and Prince Hall, one of the earliest activists in the free black community at turn of the 19th century.

The height of the ground here makes it an ideal vantage point for viewing the harbor and the Bunker Hill Monument (below) beyond in Charlestown. The British thought so too, and used this spot to fire across the way with cannons during the Battle of Bunker Hill.

On the other side of the Charlestown Bridge, the Freedom Trail continues with the **USS *Constitution***, moored at the **Charlestown Navy Yard**. "Old Ironsides", as she came to be known, was put into service in 1797 and fought her first battle in the Caribbean against the French during the war of 1812. It was the ship's strength in repelling cannonballs that earned her the enduring nickname.

Also in the Navy Yard, the **USS *Constitution* Museum** illustrates the ship's history through a vast collection of artifacts and interactive exhibits. The Charlestown Navy Yard, itself a national historic site, was actively used for shipbuilding for nearly 200 years.

On June 17th, 1775, the first formal battle of the Revolution, known as the Battle of Bunker Hill, took place. Dedicated in 1843, the **Bunker Hill Monument** commemorates this bloody battle. The 221ft (67m) obelisk contains nearly 300 steps (there is no elevator) which affords those with the endurance a spectacular view of Boston Harbor. Adjacent to the monument, there is an information center where you can find out more about the battle through exhibits and knowledgeable park rangers.

Following the devastation of Charlestown in the Battle of Bunker Hill, **Warren Tavern** *(2 Pleasant Street, ☎ 241-8142)* was the first building to be reconstructed. The tavern, dating from 1780, boasts an impressive roster of past guests, including Paul Revere and George Washington.

Bunker Hill Monument

Monument Square
☎ 242-5641
www.nps.gov/bost
🕓 Monument: Mon-Sun:
9am-4.30pm.
🕓 Exhibit Lodge:
Mon-Sun: 9am-5pm.
Admission free.

Bunker Hill Monument

Commonwealth Avenue

Newbury Street

Boylston Street

Charles River Esplanade

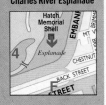

Hatch Memorial Shell

Back Bay, the South End and the Fens

Looking at **Back Bay** today, it's difficult to believe that less than 150 years ago this area consisted of nothing but marshland, the back waters of the Charles River. When Boston outgrew itself in the mid-19th century, the land west of the Boston Common was filled in, and the Back Bay neighborhood was born. A dam that had been created in the early 1800s to separate the Charles River from the Back Bay became Beacon Street, and little-by-little the areas described below were created.

This massive undertaking took more than 30 years to complete and trainloads of stone which arrived daily from nearby Needham. The project provided a unique opportunity for Boston's city planners, who took advantage of the open space to create an organized neighborhood of grand boulevards, based on those of Paris. Unlike Paris, however, the streets were laid in a grid pattern with five main boulevards intersected by eight side streets cleverly named in alphabetical order from Arlington to Hereford.

Since the land was filled over time from east to west, the architecture reflects the changing styles of the day and a walk down one of the major boulevards is like a walk through the second half of the 19th century.

Boston's moneyed classes, both the old and the new, flocked to the neighborhood, filling the houses as quickly as they were built. The grandest of the streets is **Commonwealth Avenue**, laid out with a grassy mall running its length. This was the street preferred by the *nouveau riche* who took the opportunity to funnel their wealth into some of the most ostentatious structures in Boston.

After the Depression, many of the houses of Back Bay were divided up into apartments which today are desirable condominiums. **Newbury Street** has evolved into Boston's premier shopping street, with every storefront an elegant boutique or restaurant. **Boylston Street** has also become a shopping street, though decidedly less fancy than neighboring Newbury. Throughout Back Bay there are some fine examples of private homes which you can admire from afar, and only a couple which are open to the public (see Gibson House Museum, page 30).

Stretching along the waterfront from the Harvard Bridge to the Longfellow Bridge, the **Charles River Esplanade** runs the length of Back Bay and Beacon Hill. The green belt makes for a pleasant harbor-front stroll, while the **Hatch Memorial Shell** is the location for many summertime concerts.

The best starting place for a tour of Back Bay is at the **Boston Public Garden**. The companion piece to Boston Common, with Charles Street dividing the two, the Public Garden, like Back Bay, is a man-made creation. The centerpiece is a 4 acre (1.6 hectare) pond which offers the popular activity of renting the unique "swan boats" and pedaling your way across the water. Another attraction worth noting is the 1941 sculpture series of a Mrs. Mallard and her eight ducklings, all in a row, marching through the park.

Throughout the Public Garden are statuaries and monuments to some of Boston's greatest historical figures, set within a landscape of perhaps the finest formal plantings in town.

Leaving the park from the southwest corner, you will first reach Arlington Street. The first church and one of the first buildings to be constructed in Back Bay, **Arlington Street Church** was built in 1861 according to the designs of Arthur Gilman, the architect who also laid out the neighborhood. The style is predominately Georgian, with some Italianate details, but most notable are the many Tiffany stained-glass windows.

Boston Public Garden

Arlington Street Church

351 Boylston Street
Ⓜ Arlington
☎ 536-7050
🕙 Mon-Fri: 10am-5pm.
Sun service at 11am.
Admission free.

Swan boats in the Boston Public Garden

Boston Public Garden

Church of the Covenant

67 Newbury Street
Ⓜ Arlington
☎ 266-7480
🕐 Mon-Thu: 11am-
3.30pm. Sun service:
10am.
Admission free.

Emmanuel Church of Boston

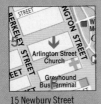

15 Newbury Street
Ⓜ Arlington
☎ 536-3355
🕐 Mon-Thu: 10am-4pm
by appointment only. Sun
service at 10am.
Admission free.

Another place to marvel at magnificent Tiffany stained-glass windows is the 1867 **Church of the Covenant** where you will find more of these windows than anywhere else in the world. In addition, an enormous Tiffany lighting fixture dangles from the magical heights of the ceiling.

The **Emmanuel Church of Boston** was built just a year later and was the first building on Newbury Street. The Gothic-style Episcopal church has wonderful acoustics. Music is so much a staple here that there is a well-respected group, Emmanuel Music, dedicated to performing at the church throughout the year. Note the Leslie Lindsey Chapel, a memorial to a young woman whose honeymoon voyage on the *Lusitania* was her last.

Walking up Arlington, you will pass the **Ritz-Carlton** which, with the **Four Seasons Hotel** on the other side of the Public Garden, are the two premier hotels in Boston. Although the Four Seasons is a modern building with every convenience imaginable, the 1927 Ritz-Carlton epitomizes white-glove service and elegance. *(Ritz-Carlton: 15 Arlington Street,* Ⓜ *Arlington,* ☎ *(800) 241-3333. Four Seasons Hotel: 200 Boylston Street,* ☎ *(800) 338-4400.)*

Situated one block from the Public Garden, on Beacon Street, the **Gibson House Museum** provides visitors with a glimpse of the home life of a prominent Boston family during Victorian times. Built in 1859 for Catherine Hammond Gibson, the Italian Renaissance Revival-style townhouse served as the family home for three generations of Gibsons before opening to the public as a house museum in 1957. Designed by celebrated local architect Edward Clark Cabot, the Gibson house was built of brownstone and red brick and has the distinction of being one of the earliest houses to be built in Back Bay.

Tours of the interior include the grand, public spaces of the home, tastefully furnished in the style of the day, as well as service areas such as the kitchen and laundry which provide additional clues to the lifestyle of an upper middle-class family during the Victorian period.

Built in 1872 in the Romanesque Revival style, the **First Baptist Church** was designed by the architect Henry Hobson Richardson who also designed the better-known Trinity Church (page 32). The frieze covering the tower was crafted by sculptor Frédéric Auguste Bartholdi, famous for a somewhat more significant project – the Statue of Liberty.

The enormous **Exeter Street Theater** was originally designed as a place of worship in 1884. For most of the 20th century, it functioned as a movie house where it was especially popular during long runs of the *Rocky Horror Picture Show*. Today it houses a restaurant and a bookstore. *(26 Exeter Street,* Ⓜ *Copley.)*

Copley Square, the heart of Back Bay, is the location of many festivals and fairs throughout the year, as well as being the finish line of the Boston Marathon.

Dominating the square is the **Boston Public Library**, the country's oldest, containing a collection of more than 7 million books, many of them rare or important historical documents. Built in 1895 by the venerated team of McKim, Mead and White, the dramatic building boasts an interior of palatial halls and staircases, splendid reading rooms and courtyard gardens, embellished with incredible murals by artists such as John Singer Sargent and Puvis de Chavannes.

The centerpiece of the library is Bates

Gibson House Museum

137 Beacon Street
☎ 267-6338
Ⓜ Arlington
🕑 Tours: May-Nov: Wed-Sun: 1pm, 2pm and 3pm. Nov-May: Sat-Sun: 1pm, 2pm and 3pm. Admission charge.
2 admissions for the price of 1 with voucher on page 65.

First Baptist Church

110 Commonwealth Avenue
Ⓜ Copley
☎ 267-3148
🕑 Mon-Fri: 10am-4pm by appointment only. Sun service: 11am.

Boston Public Library

700 Boylston Street
Ⓜ Copley
☎ 536-5400
🕑 Mon-Thu: 9am-9pm. Fri-Sat: 9am-5pm. Sun: 1pm-5pm.
Admission free.

206 Clarendon Street
Ⓜ Copley
☎ 536-0944.
🕒 Mon-Sun: 8am-6pm
plus Sunday services.
Admission free.

**John Hancock
Tower**

Copley Square
Ⓜ Copley Square
☎ 247-1977
www.jhancock.com/
company/observatory/
🕒 Apr-Oct: Mon-Sun:
9am-10pm. Nov-Mar:
Mon-Sat: 9am-10pm.
Sun: 9am-5pm.
Admission charge.
**2 admissions for the
price of 1 with voucher
on page 65. Discount not
applicable on July 4th.**

"New" Old South Church

645 Boylston Street
Ⓜ Copley
☎ 536-1970
🕒 Mon-Fri: 9am-5pm.
Sat: 9am-3pm. Sun
service 11am (10am in
summer).
Admission free.

Hall, a room that is more than 200ft
(60m) long and topped with an enormous
barrel ceiling, reaching a lofty 50ft (15m).

Across from the library is the imposing
Trinity Church. The pinnacle of a lifetime's
work for architect Henry Hobson
Richardson, the 1877 Romanesque
Revival-style church is considered by many
to be a masterpiece. The design is based
on the 11th-century Romanesque
churches in France, and the proportions
used are remarkable.

Inside, lush paintings and stained glass by
the masters of the day shine in colored
brilliance. The decorated organ pipes are
a particular highlight, as are the free
organ concerts held here on Fridays at
12.15pm.

An incredible sight is Trinity Church's
reflection in the sheer face of its neighbor,
the I.M. Pei-designed **John Hancock
Tower**. The tallest building in New England
is amazing enough from the ground where
it towers above the nearby buildings, but
the view from the **Observatory**, 740ft
(225m) high, is unbeatable. Enter the
building at Trinity Place and St. James
Avenue, and head for the express elevator
which whisks you 60 floors into the air.

From the Observatory, you can enjoy a
panoramic view of Boston and beyond.
From the south-facing floor-to-ceiling
windows, you get great views of Boston
Harbor and the Atlantic Ocean, stretching
along the coastline towards Cape Cod. To
the east, you'll see Logan Airport, Quincy
Market and the gold dome of the
Massachusetts State House with the
Boston Public Garden and Boston
Common spread out before it.

On a clear day, views to the north can
stretch as far as New Hampshire and
Vermont, with Cambridge and the Charles
River in the foreground. To the west, see
the Back Bay and the illuminated stadium
Fenway Park (page 36), home of the
Boston Red Sox.

Several exhibits in the Observatory
illustrate the view with descriptions of the
attractions laid out before you. The "Road
to Independence" exhibit uses special

effects, music and a miniature model city to take you back to Boston's colonial times, where you can witness events like the Boston Tea Party, the Battle of Bunker Hill and Paul Revere's ride.

Placed throughout the Observatory are illuminated photographs of historic and present-day landmarks accompanied by fact-filled text. "Aviation Radio" taps you into the live radio transmissions between planes and the tower at Logan Airport. There are also computer exhibits, telescopes and a gift shop with souvenirs of Boston and the tower.

Trinity Church and the John Hancock Tower

The strangely-named **"New" Old South Church** became the new building for the congregation of the Old South Meeting House (page 13) in 1875. The ornate Gothic design is a stark contrast to the simple design of the meeting house.

Nearby, you can shop to your heart's content at the elegant **Copley Place**, crossing the glass walkway to reach the adjacent **Prudential Center**, the larger of the two indoor shopping malls (see *Shopping*, pages 52-53). Also connected to the "Pru", as it is known, is the **Hynes Convention Center** *(900 Boylston, ☎ 954-2000)* which can hold events for more than 20,000 people.

High above the sprawling complex, the 52-story **Prudential Tower** has several places from which to observe the view, including a restaurant and an observatory, the **Prudential Center Skywalk**, on the 50th floor.

Next to the Prudential Center, the **Christian Science Church Center** occupies nearly 14 acres (6.5 hectares). The world

Prudential Center

800 Boylston Street
Ⓜ Prudential
☎ 236-2366
🕐 Mon-Sat: 10am-8pm.
Sun: 11am-6pm.
Admission free.
Skywalk:
☎ 859-0648
🕐 Mon-Sun: 10am-10pm.
Admission charge.

Christian Science Church Center

175 Avenue of the Arts
Ⓜ Prudential
☎ 450-3790
🕐 Church: Tue-Sat:
10am-4pm. Sun:
11.15am-2pm.
Tours free.
Mapparium:
🕐 Closed for renovation
until 2001.

Symphony Hall

301 Massachusetts Avenue
Ⓜ Symphony
☎ 266-1492

headquarters for the Christian Science Faith has a "mother" church that seats 3,000. The original church was constructed in 1894 and has been expanded several times. Also on the property is a vast reflecting pool, an office complex designed by I.M. Pei in 1973 to house the administration.

One of the biggest draws to the complex is the **Mapparium**, a stained-glass globe built in the 1930s that spans over 30ft (9m). It is located in the building which houses the Christian Science Publishing Society, publishers of the well-known *Christian Science Monitor*, but has recently been closed for renovations. Call ahead for details of its reopening.

Completed in 1900, **Symphony Hall** is another magnificent achievement for the architectural firm of McKim, Mead and White. With its excellent acoustics, it is said that there isn't a bad seat in the house – no small task considering that there are more than 2,500. Not only is this the home of the Boston Symphony Orchestra, but it also hosts concerts by the Boston Pops and various other performers.

Situated across from the convention center, the **Institute of Contemporary Art** is housed in a building dating to 1886, originally used as a police station. Rotating exhibits showcase contemporary artists in all variety of media and ensure that a visit to the ICA always provides something fresh.

Northeastern University, founded in 1898, is a true urban university. It lacks a formal campus, and is rather indistinctly smudged into the area that surrounds it. Academically, the university's strong suit is its cooperative education program which allows students to work in their field while earning their degree.

Renoir's Dance at Bougival, *Museum of Fine Arts*

Before the Back Bay project was complete, planners handed over to Frederick Law Olmsted a large open space to be landscaped into a spectacular park. As he did with his masterpiece, New York's Central Park, he fashioned a green space mainly by keeping much of the land in its natural state and embellishing it in such a way as to bring out its greatest beauty. The **Back Bay Fens**, or simply the Fens, is considered the first of the "**Emerald Necklace**", a string of Olmsted spaces stretching from here into the suburbs.

Overlooking the Fens, the **Museum of Fine Arts** is one of Boston's premier attractions, and one of the world's most important museums. Before you even sample a taste of the vast collection presented here, you will know by the grand edifice that you are somewhere special. The imposing Beaux Arts structure contains all the tell-tale signs of an important museum – majestic staircases, high ceilings, great frescoed domes and so on. The I.M. Pei-designed West Wing, added in 1981, allowed the museum to expand its exhibit space in a modern and practical manner.

The original collection was founded in 1876, and relocated here in 1909 when it outgrew its previous space in Copley Square. It represents many important European schools, including the Impressionists, but is also devoted in part to American works. It is, in fact, one of the best collections of American art in the country. The MFA also has the largest group of Monets outside Paris, as well as renowned collections of Egyptian, Asian and Classical art.

Nearby, visitors will find the **Isabella Stewart Gardner Museum** one of the most extraordinary house museums they have ever seen. The brazen socialite shocked proper Bostonians when she arrived on the scene in 1860, following her marriage to John Lowell Gardner. She used her own massive fortune and that of her husband to acquire the prestigious art collection you see today.

The Venetian-style "palazzo" she named Fenway Court was built to impress, and impress it did. Guests could mingle in the

Institute of Contemporary Art

955 Boylston Street
Ⓜ Hynes Convention Center
☎ 266-5152
🕐 Wed-Thu & Sat-Sun: 12noon-5pm. Fri: 12noon-7pm. Mon-Tue: closed.
Admission charge.
2 admissions for the price of 1 with voucher on page 65.

Northeastern University

360 Avenue of the Arts
Ⓜ Northeastern
☎ 373-2000

Museum of Fine Arts

465 Avenue of the Arts
Ⓜ Museum of Fine Arts
☎ 267-9300
www.mfa.org
🕐 Mon-Tue and Sat-Sun: 10am-4.45pm. Wed-Fri: 10am-9.45pm.
Admission charge.
$2 off admission charge with voucher on page 65.

Isabella Stewart Gardner Museum

280 The Fenway
Ⓜ Museum of Fine Arts
☎ 566-1401
🕐 Tue-Sun: 11am-5pm.
Mon: closed.
Admission charge.

Fenway Park

4 Yawkley Way
Ⓜ Kenmore
☎ 267-1700 for tickets,
☎ 236-6666 for tours
🕐 Tour hours vary, so
call ahead for details.
Admission charge.

Photographic Resource Center

602 Commonwealth Ave
Ⓜ Blandford
☎ 353-0700
www.bu.edu/prc/
Gallery: 🕐 Tue-Wed and
Fri-Sun: 12noon-5pm.
Thu: 12noon-8pm. Mon:
closed.
Library: 🕐 Tue & Sat:
12noon-5pm. Thu:
12noon-8pm. Fri, Sun-
Mon & Wed: closed.
Admission charge.
**2 admissions for the
price of 1 with voucher
on page 67.**

glass-roofed central courtyard, surrounded by treasures of art dripping from the walls and incredible sculptures guarding her palace. She remained in her beloved home until her death in 1924. The terms of her legacy dictated that absolutely everything in the home would remain exactly as it was while she was alive. A visitor couldn't be happier with her decision.

On the other side of the Fens is the aptly named baseball stadium, **Fenway Park**, home of the Boston Red Sox. The 1912 stadium is expected soon to go the way of the old Boston Garden (page 22) and be replaced by a newer facility, so diehard baseball buffs will want to catch it while they can. The best way to do this is to take the guided tour.

Nearby **Kenmore Square** reflects the interests of the local student population with a profusion of cheap restaurants and cafés, trendy bars and late-night clubs. The party continues along **Lansdowne Street**, one of Boston's main destinations for club-going.

Following Commonwealth Avenue from Kenmore Square, you will come upon the dense campus of **Boston University**. Like Northeastern, the campus is not self-contained, but rather blends in with the city around it. The university has earned a reputation for turning out literary stars. The roster includes Sylvia Plath, Anne Sexton and Pulitzer-prize winners Elie Weisel and Saul Bellow.

Boston University is home to a strong theater group as well as several notable art galleries, including the **Photographic Resource Center**, founded in 1976. Changing exhibitions at the center, supplemented by lectures, workshops and a 4,000-volume library, cover everything from historic and contemporary photos to a philosophical examination of the role played by photography in human experience.

The **South End**, man-made like Back Bay, was also a desirable place to live when it was first created. Like many neighborhoods in urban areas throughout the U.S., the 20th century saw the district's decline. Only recently has the decay begun to be washed away by the tides of gentrification. An excellent example of this is the lovely **Union Park**. Laid out in 1851, the square reflects the genteel tastes of Victorian Boston, with its wrought-iron fences and graceful brownstones. *(Between Shawmut and Tremont Streets.* Ⓜ *Back Bay.)*

Just around the corner, on Tremont Street, is the city-supported **Boston Center for the Arts**. A favorite amongst locals, the complex is the place to go when seeking art and culture that may be a little out of the ordinary. The 1884 building, originally called the Cyclorama (a moniker Bostonians refuse to entirely let go), encompasses three theaters, a gallery and a separate studio space.

Built in 1875 in the Gothic Revival style, the **Cathedral of the Holy Cross** is the largest Roman Catholic church in New England and the seat of New England's cardinal. When the Pope visited the U.S. in 1979, this was one of his stops.

Back towards the Public Garden, the tiny, quaint streets of **Bay Village** seem like an anomaly in this bustling district, wedged between the many busy streets surrounding it. The unique atmosphere has led to an influx of artists and creative types, and the area is also characterized as being a center of gay life in Boston. *(Between Arlington, Stuart and Charles Streets.* Ⓜ *Arlington/Boylston.)*

Adjacent is the **Theater District**, centered around Tremont Street, which also borders Chinatown. In addition to the many theaters located here (see *Nightlife*, pages 54-55), there are also plenty of cafés, restaurants and clubs.

Boston Center for the Arts

539 Tremont Street
Ⓜ Back Bay
☎ 426-5000
⏱ Hours vary, call ahead for details.
Admission free.

Cathedral of the Holy Cross

1400 Washington Street
Ⓜ Back Bay
☎ 542-5682
⏱ Mon-Sat: 9am-3pm. Sun: 8am-3pm. Sun service: 8am and 11am.
Admission free.

A Boston Red Sox baseball game

Beyond Central Boston

Within the greater Boston area, but beyond the city's main neighborhoods, there is a wealth of attractions. Across the Charles River there is **Cambridge** and the neighboring areas of **Allston** and **Somerville**. Beyond Back Bay and the Fens, lie the elegant suburbs of **Brookline**, **Roxbury** and **South Boston**. Historic **Quincy** is just 20 minutes away. These destinations are all easily accessible by public transport.

Long considered Boston's "Left Bank", **Cambridge** is a college town and more. When it was founded as Newtowne in 1630, it was essentially a Puritan farming community. It was renamed Cambridge soon after for the English university where many of its leaders were educated. Officially a city since 1846, today's Cambridge is home to two of the nation's most prestigious universities – Harvard University (page 39) and the Massachusetts Institute of Technology (page 43), and much of the town's character is derived from its connections to university life. Evidence of this is found in the many bookstores, inexpensive eateries and bars that line the streets. It also boasts some fine historic homes and world-class museums.

Harvard Square

Harvard Univerity

Harvard Square

Cambridge maintains a village-like atmosphere, in part because of the organization of the streets around "squares". All roads seem to lead to one or the other of these hubs, and none is more famous than **Harvard Square**. In warm weather, the streets are jammed with pedestrians bombarded by the sounds of street musicians plying their trade. In any weather, the cafés and shops along the square and the surrounding streets are packed with students, tourists and locals soaking up their share of the Cambridge atmosphere. Right by the T station is the bustling **Out of Town News**, the best place to pick up periodicals from around the world.

Steps from Harvard Square is **Harvard University**, arguably the premier university in the nation. Founded in 1636, Harvard College was later dubbed the "cradle of higher education" for the significant role it played in the early development of academics in this country.

Historic buildings, the earliest of which dates to 1720, surround the picturesque **Harvard Yard**, centerpiece of the campus and a first stop for visitors. The next oldest building in the yard is the delicate, yellow-clapboard 1726 **Wadsworth House**, the front of which faces Massachusetts Avenue.

The original Harvard College was named for clergyman **John Harvard**, whose statue has stood in Harvard Yard since 1848. Judging by the constant click of cameras, it is possibly the biggest tourist draw at the university. Behind the statue is the imposing 1813 **University Hall**, designed by Charles Bulfinch. Another campus behemoth is **Widener Library**, situated in the square behind University Hall. The library was constructed from the $2 million donation of the Widener family whose Harvard-educated son drowned when the *Titanic* sank.

Many visitors to the campus seek out the distinguished **Harvard University Art Museums**. Together, the collections amount to more than 150,000 works distributed amongst several museums.

The **Fogg Art Museum** was founded in 1895, and has occupied its current building since 1927. It houses European art from the Middle Ages to the present day as well as American art from the 16th to the 20th centuries. The collection is displayed in a series of rooms opening off a central courtyard constructed of Italian stone.

Exiting the Fogg through Werner Otto Hall, you will reach the **Busch-Reisinger Museum** of central and northern European art. The museum is especially strong in its 20th-century German collection.

Wadsworth House

Widener Library

Harvard University Art Museums
Fogg Art Museum

32 Quincy Street,
Cambridge

Busch-Reisinger Museum:
32 Quincy Street,
Cambridge

Arthur M. Sackler Museum:
485 Broadway,
Cambridge

☎ 495-9400
🕐 Mon-Sat: 10am-5pm.
Sun: 1pm-5pm.
Admission charge
includes entrance to all
museums. Free
admission Wed: 10am-
5pm and Sat: 10am-
12noon.

Fogg Art Museum

Semetic Museum

6 Divinity Avenue, Camb.
Ⓜ Harvard
☎ 495-4631
🕐 Mon-Fri: 10am-4pm.
Sat: closed. Sun: 1pm-
4pm.
Admission free.

for less **Harvard Museum of Natural History**

26 Oxford Street, Camb.
Ⓜ Harvard
☎ 495-3045
www.hmnh.harvard.edu
🕐 Mon-Sat: 9am-5pm.
Sun: 1pm-5pm.
Admission charge also
includes admission to
the Peabody Museum.
2 admissions for the price of 1 with voucher of page 67.

The **Arthur M. Sackler Museum** presents much earlier art. Asian and Islamic art are the primary focus, but art from other cultures is also exhibited, including Greek and Roman sculpture.

The **Semetic Museum**, founded in 1889, houses Harvard's Near Eastern archeological collections. More than 40,000 ancient artifacts have been gathered from expeditions to Egypt, Israel, Cyprus and beyond to comprise the collections housed here. Free lectures and tours enhance a visit to the museum and provide visitors with information on all facets of Near Eastern archeology, history and culture.

The **Harvard Museum of Natural History** features the university's vast and outstanding natural history collection, organized into three main galleries. The highlight of the **botanical galleries** is the famous Ware Collection of Blaschka Glass Models of Plants. More commonly referred to as the "Glass Flowers", these models number more than 3,000 and were created from 1886 to 1937 by the father and son team Leopold and Rudolph Blaschka. From prehistoric life forms to the creatures with whom we share our world today, the **zoological galleries** provide specimens from the animal world, while the **mineralogical galleries** display geological finds from meteorites to sparkling gems. Don't miss the recently acquired 1,642lb (745kg) amethyst geode from Brazil.

Adjoining the Harvard Museum of Natural History, the **Peabody Museum of Archaeology and Ethnology** provides an opportunity to examine collections and current issues in anthropology at one of the most renowned museums of its kind worldwide. The **Hall of the North American Indian** is a must-see, with its vast collection of artifacts representing a wide range of native cultures. *Encounters with the Americas* focuses on Mesoamerican natives and the effects contact with Europeans had on their lives and culture.

Between Massachusetts Avenue and Garden Street sprawls 16-acre (6.5 hectare) **Cambridge Common**. Formed in 1621, it is the only bit of colonial Cambridge to remain today. During the years leading up to the Revolution, it was the site where George Washington took control of his army under the tree nicknamed the "Washington Elm", today marked by a plaque. Two years later, William Dawes rode through here with Revere and Prescott (page 8) to warn the patriots that the British troops were coming. Across Garden Street, the traffic island is named **Dawes Island** in his memory.

On the other side of Cambridge Common is **Radcliffe Yard**. It is part of the campus of **Radcliffe College**, founded in 1879 as a college for women. Nearly a century later, Radcliffe officially merged with Harvard University, though it maintains some degree of autonomy. Today, the college accepts male students, but gender studies are still a special focus. *(Bordered by Appian Way, Garden, Mason and Brattle Streets.)*

Christ Church, the oldest church in Cambridge, dates to 1761, and counted George and Martha Washington among its congregation. Visitors interested in attending a service here should call ahead as times vary throughout the year.

Nearby is the **Old Burying Ground**, founded in 1635. This colonial cemetery is the final resting place for mostly 17th- and 18th-century Cambridge residents, ranging from Revolutionary War soldiers to Harvard University presidents.

Brattle Street stretches out from Harvard

Peabody Museum of Archaeology and Ethnology

11 Divinity Avenue, Cambridge
Ⓜ Harvard
☎ 496-1027
www.peabody.harvard.edu
🕐 Mon-Sat: 9am-5pm.
Sun: 1pm-5pm.
Admission charge also includes admission to the Harvard Museum of Natural History.
2 admissions for the price of 1 with voucher of page 67.

Christ Church

0 Garden Street, Cambridge
Ⓜ Harvard
☎ 876-0200
🕐 Mon-Fri and Sun: 7.30am-6pm.
Sat: 7.30am-3pm.
Admission free.

Old Burying Ground

Massachusetts Avenue, Cambridge
Ⓜ Harvard
☎ 349-4683
🕐 Mon-Sun: dawn to dusk.
Admission free.

Brattle House

42 Brattle Street,
Cambridge
Ⓜ Harvard
☎ 547-6789 ext. 239
🕐 Mon-Thu: 9am-9pm.
Fri: 9am-7pm. Sat: 9am-
2pm. Sun: closed.
Admission free.

Dexter Pratt House

56 Brattle Street,
Cambridge
Ⓜ Harvard
☎ 547-6789
🕐 Mon-Sat: 9am-6pm.
Sun: closed.
Admission free.

**Longfellow National
Historic Site**

105 Brattle Street,
Cambridge
Ⓜ Harvard
☎ 876-4492
🕐 Closed for
renovations until late
2001/early 2002. Call
ahead for details on
reopening.

Square, passing through some of Radcliffe
College's campus. The historic homes that
line this street, with their clapboard fronts
and classic proportions, provide fantastic
examples of colonial residential
architecture and make a walk here one of
the most pleasant in Cambridge. Brattle
Street is nick-named Tory Row for the
royalists who owned homes here until after
the Revolutionary War when they were
forced to leave.

Walking along Brattle Street away from
Harvard Square, the first house you will
encounter is **Brattle House**, one of the
seven Tory homes on Tory Row. Named
after first owner William Brattle, number 42
was occupied by feminist editor Margaret
Fuller in the 1830s. A few doors down, the
Dexter Pratt House achieved fame as the
blacksmith's home in Longfellow's poem
The Village Blacksmith (see below).

Vassall House, at number 94, belonged to
loyalist Henry Vassall during the mid-18th
century, though the structure was
probably built much earlier. During the
Revolution, as was the case with many of
the houses deserted by Tories, it served a
practical purpose. In this instance, it was
a hospital. *(94 Brattle Street. 🕐 Closed to the
public.)*

The most famous house on the street
occupies number 105 and is known as the
Longfellow National Historic Site. Built in
1750, the house was used from 1775-
1776 by George Washington during the
siege of Boston. In 1837, the poet and
Harvard professor Henry Wadsworth
Longfellow came to live here as a boarder.
He later married the daughter of a wealthy
mill-owner, and his new father-in-law
purchased the house for the couple. The
poet, along with his wife and eventually
their six children, lived here until his death
in 1882. It was here that many of his most
famous poems were written, including *Paul
Revere's Ride*. Unfortunately, the house is
closed for renovation, but you can pick up
a brochure by the outside gate and explore
the grounds.

At number 159, the **Hooper-Lee-Nichols
House** is the oldest in Cambridge, dating
to 1688. It now houses the Cambridge

Historical Society and visiting hours are limited, so please note the times below.

West of the Harvard Square area, on Mount Auburn Street, is the 174-acre **Mount Auburn Cemetery**. Almost 90,000 people are buried at Mount Auburn, including Henry Wadsworth Longfellow, Charles Bulfinch and Winslow Homer. *(580 Mount Auburn Street,* Ⓜ *Harvard,* ☎ *547-7105.* ⏲ *Mon-Sun: 8am-5pm. Admission free.)*

Traveling east of Harvard Square, you will reach the internationally flavored **Central Square**. Ethnic restaurants abound and it is one of the best places for live music in the Boston area (see *Nightlife*, pages 54-55). Also located here is Cambridge City Hall.

Further east, towards Boston proper, **Kendall Square** is the haunt of students from the other major Cambridge university, the **Massachusetts Institute of Technology**, or MIT. Enjoying a reputation as one of the world's premier think-tanks for the sciences, since the Second World War MIT has made essential contributions in the fields of space exploration, bioengineering, new media and information technology, among others. Founded in 1861 in Boston's Copley Square, the school relocated to its current location on the Charles River in 1916. The majority of the neoclassical architecture dates to this period, but there are also examples of modern architecture, such as I.M. Pei's Green Building and Wiesner Building. There is also an abundance of outdoor sculpture on campus, including works by Alexander Calder and Pablo Picasso. In addition to visiting the MIT Museum

Hooper-Lee-Nichols House

159 Brattle Street, Cambridge
Ⓜ Harvard
☎ 547-4252
⏲ Open for tours only.
Tue and Thu: 2pm-5pm.
Wed and Fri-Mon: closed.
Admission charge.

Massachusetts Institute of Technology

Information Center: 77 Massachusetts Avenue, Cambridge
Ⓜ Kendall/MIT
☎ 253-4795
⏲ Free tours: Mon-Fri: 10am and 2pm.

Longfellow National Historic Site

Shooting the Apple, *1964, MIT Museum*

MIT Museum

Main Exhibition Center:
265 Massachusetts Ave,
Cambridge
Ⓜ Kendall/MIT
☎ 253-4444
www.mit.edu/museum
🕐 Tue-Fri: 10am-5pm.
Sat-Sun: 12noon-5pm.
Admission charge.
2 admissions for the price of 1 with voucher on page 67.

John F. Kennedy's birthplace and childhood home

83 Beals Street,
Brookline
Ⓜ Coolidge Corner
☎ 566-7937
🕐 Apr-Nov: Wed-Sun:
10am-4.30pm. Mon-Tue:
closed. Dec-mid-Mar:
closed.
Admission charge.

(below), visitors may take a free guided tour of the campus.

The **MIT Museum** documents MIT's role in 19th and 20th-century science and technology through an extensive collection of art, drawings, artifacts, photographs and instruments. Of special note are the collections in architecture, nautical history and holography. The collection is displayed in three primary exhibition spaces. The Main Exhibition Center features the world's largest holography collection, the Hall of Hacks, a tribute to the ingenuity of MIT grads, and rotating exhibits in science and technology. The Hart Nautical Gallery *(Building 5, 77 Massachusetts Avenue)* displays exceptional ship models and changing exhibits on the history of naval architecture, shipbuilding and design. The Compton Gallery *(Building 10)* mounts exhibitions illustrating the interaction between science and art.

Almost completely surrounded by the Charles River, the funky neighborhood of **Allston** is a short walk from Harvard Square (page 38) via the Lars Anderson Bridge. The area is rife with discount clothing stores, hip restaurants and hot nightspots, centered on Harvard Avenue, the main thoroughfare (see also *Shopping* and *Nightlife*, pages 52-55). Allston is also the location of Harvard's business school.

Once part of neighboring Charlestown (page 24), **Somerville** became a city of its own in 1842. Basically a working-class town, Somerville has slowly begun to draw an alternative, young crowd attracted by its cheap rents. The best example of this process is seen around **Davis Square**, where you can find hip clothing stores, record shops and funky restaurants.

Traveling west from Boston's Kenmore Square (page 36), you will encounter the suburb of **Brookline**. Besides having some great restaurants and pubs, it also contains some historic sights. **John F. Kennedy's birthplace and childhood home** is located here, as is the **home and office of Frederick Law Olmsted**, the famed landscape architect. Both are national historic sites.

Isabel and Larz Anderson were an ultra-wealthy Boston couple who, at the start of the 20th century, shared a passion for the new world of motor cars. Part of their estate became Larz Anderson Park, and the original 1889 Anderson family Carriage House was converted into the **Museum of Transportation**. The mahogany and brick structure first housed the Anderson horses and carriages, and later their collection of automobiles. Today, many of their cars are on display, including a steam-powered 1903 Gardner-Serpollet and one of the country's first racing cars, a 1901 Winton. The collection is supplemented by seasonal exhibits and family memorabilia. The museum also hosts special events.

In nearby Chestnut Hill, **Boston College** is one of the country's first Jesuit universities, founded in 1863. It has an excellent reputation for both its academic studies and its athletics. *(40 Commonwealth Avenue, Chestnut Hill, ☎ 552-8000.)*

The area of Jamaica Plain is located in southwest Boston and is home to 120-acre (48 hectare) **Jamaica Pond**. Part of Olmsted's "Emerald Necklace" (page 35), the pond is a great place for a stroll, picnic or a boat ride. In warm weather, people gather by the bandstand to hear jazz and classical music. *Jamaicaway, Jamaica Plain, ☎ 635-7383.)*

Nearby is the lovely **Arnold Arboretum**, also designed by Olmsted. This huge expanse of land is home to more than 15,000 species of trees and shrubs.

Also in Jamaica Plain is the **Loring-Greenough House**, former home of

---

Home and office of Frederick Law Olmsted

99 Warren Street, Brookline
Ⓜ Brookline Hills
☎ 566-1689
🕐 Fri-Sun: 10am-4.30pm. Mon-Thu: closed.
Admission free.

Museum of Transportation

15 Newton Street, Brookline
Ⓜ Reservoir/Forest Hills/Cleveland Circle, then bus 51
☎ 522-6547
www.mot.org
🕐 Tue-Sun: 10am-5pm. Mon: closed.
Admission charge.
2 admissions for the price of 1 with voucher on page 67.

Museum of Transportation

Arnold Arboretum

135 Arborway, Jamaica Plain
Ⓜ Forest Hills
☎ 524-1718
🕐 Mon-Sun: dawn-dusk.
Admission free.

Shirley-Eustis House

for less

33 Shirley Street, Roxbury
Ⓜ Ruggles, then bus 15
☎ 442-2275
www.shirleyeustishouse.org
🕐 Thu-Sun: 12noon-4pm.
Mon-Wed: closed.
Admission charge.
2 admissions for the price of 1 with voucher on page 67.

Museum of the National Center of Afro-American Artists

for less

300 Walnut Avenue, Roxbury
Ⓜ Ruggles
☎ 442-8614
🕐 Tue-Sun: 1pm-5pm.
Mon: closed.
Admission charge.
2 admissions for the price of 1 with voucher on page 67.

royalist Joshua Loring. Today you can visit the home that was also used as a hospital for George Washington's troops. *(12 South Street, Jamaica Plain,* Ⓜ *Freen Street/Forest Hills,* ☎ *524-3158.* 🕐 *Tours by appointment. Donation suggested.)*

Following the "Emerald Necklace", the next, and perhaps best, jewel is huge **Franklin Park**. Rolling lawns with incredible vistas, woodlands and a golf course are some of the highlights of this country park. The **Franklin Park Zoo** is also located here. *(1 Franklin Park Road,* Ⓜ *Forest Hills,* ☎ *635-7383.* 🕐 *Park: Mon-Sun: dawn to dusk. Zoo: Winter: Mon-Sun: 10am-4pm. Summer: Mon-Fri: 10am-6pm. Sat-Sun: 10am-6pm. Admission charge for zoo only.)*

The Georgian mansion known today as the **Shirley-Eustis House** is the only remaining country house in America built by a British royal colonial governor. It was erected from 1747-1751 by William Shirley, who was appointed royal governor of Massachusetts Bay Colony and Commander-in-Chief of all British forces in North America by George II. It later became the home of William Eustis, Governor of the Commonwealth of Massachusetts, from 1823-1825. Esteemed figures such as George Washington, the Marquis de Lafayette and Benjamin Franklin paid visits to this landmark home. Today, visitors can get a first-hand look at this restored historical gem.

Also in Roxbury is the **Museum of the National Center of Afro-American Artists**. The museum pays tribute to the arts legacy created by African-Americans and African descendants worldwide.

The **John F. Kennedy Library and Museum** is a must-see for any visitor with an interest in the Kennedy legacy or American history in general. Housed in a striking building designed by I.M. Pei, adjacent to the University of Massachusetts Boston campus, the library and museum capture the dynamism and youthful spirit of one of America's most popular presidents.

Twenty-five exhibits draw on rare television and film footage, official documents and personal keepsakes to create a stirring account of Kennedy's thousand days in

John F. Kennedy Library and Museum

office, placed within the context of the American experience during this period. Visitors can witness the first televised presidential debate, glimpse life during the Cold War, feel the tension of the Cuban Missile Crisis and relive the thrill of the dawn of the space age. Follow First Lady Jacqueline Bouvier Kennedy on her televised tour of the White House and it is easy to see how this charming woman endeared herself to the nation. Before completing a visit here, stroll the 9 acre (3.6 hectare) park surrounding the complex. Situated on Columbia Point, it overlooks the waterfront and provides excellent views of the Boston skyline.

Known as the "City of Presidents", **Quincy** was the birthplace of the two John Adamses, the only father and son to serve as president.

Built by Revolutionary leader Colonel Josiah Quincy as a country estate, **Josiah Quincy House** befits the status of the prominent family that occupied it. The Quincys were pivotal in the social and political life of Massachusetts, and counted among them three mayors of Boston and a president of Harvard.

In the late 19th century, Eliza Susan Quincy took steps to ensure that the house could be a repository of family history, including persuading family members to return heirlooms to Josiah Quincy House. Architectural details such as a classical portico and a Chinese fretwork balustrade enhance the simple lines and clean design of the house.

John F. Kennedy Library and Museum

Columbia Point, Dorchester
Ⓜ JFK/UMass, then free shuttle
☎ 929-4500
www.cs.umb.edu/ jfklibrary/museum.htm
🕓 Mon-Sun: 9am-5pm. Admission charge.
2 admissions for the price of 1 with voucher on page 69.

Josiah Quincy House

20 Muirhead Street, Quincy
☎ 471-4508
www.spnea.org
🕓 Jun-mid-Oct: Sat-Sun: 11am-5pm. Last tour 4pm. Mon-Fri: closed. Mid-Oct-May: closed. Admission charge.
2 admissions for the price of 1 with voucher on page 69.

Beyond the City

The seat of the Codman family for five generations, **Codman House** in Lincoln is rich with reminders of each generation. Visitors can also stroll the grounds which feature Italianate and English gardens. *(Codman Road, ☎ (781) 259-8843. www.spnea.org ⊕ Jun-mid-Oct: Wed-Sun: 11am-5pm. Last tour 4pm. Grounds: sunrise-sunset. Mon-Tue: closed. Mid-Oct-Jun: closed. Admission charge.* **2 for the price of 1 with voucher on page 69.***)*

Walter Gropius (1883-1969) was the founder of the German Bauhaus school of design, characterized by maximum efficiency and simplicity of design. **Gropius House**, built in 1937, embodied the style and combined revolutionary materials with traditional New England wood and brick. The house contains an important collection of Marcel Breuer furniture, designed specifically for the architect. *(68 Baker Bridge Road, ☎ (781) 259-8098. www.spnea.org ⊕ Jun-mid-Oct: Wed-Sun: 11am-5pm. Last tour 4pm. Mon-Tue: closed. Mid-Oct-May: Sat-Sun: 11am-5pm. Mon-Fri: closed. Admission charge.* **2 for the price of 1 with voucher on page 69.***)*

Lexington was the site of the first battle of the Revolutionary War on April 19th, 1775. Several monuments commemorate the occasion, and the **Lexington Visitor Center** *(1875 Massachusetts Avenue, ☎ (781) 862-1450)* has a wealth of information.

Directly across from the green is the c.1690 **Buckman Tavern** *(1 Bedford Street, ☎ (781) 862-5598)*, where patriot "Minutemen" assembled on the morning of the opening battle of the American Revolution. A short walk brings you to the 1698 **Hancock-Clarke House** *(36 Hancock Street, ☎ (781) 861-0928)*, where John Hancock and Samuel Adams were sleeping when Revere and Dawes rode through warning patriots of the British soldiers' approach. Nearby is **Munroe Tavern** *(1332 Massachusetts Avenue, ☎ (781) 674-9238)*, where the British troops stopped on their retreat to Boston to

Gropius House

tend their wounded and catch their breath after the debacle at North Bridge. (www.lexingtonhistory.org ① Mid-Apr-Oct: Mon-Sat: 10am-5pm. Sun: 1pm-5pm. Nov-mid-Apr: closed. One admission charge. *2 for the price of 1 with vouchers on page 69*).

It was at the **Old North Bridge** in **Concord** where the Minutemen successfully forced the British to flee on April 19th, 1775. Within sight of the bridge is the **Old Manse**, where the Reverend William Emerson lived at the time. Today you can visit the house, which was occupied by the writer Nathaniel Hawthorne for a year in 1834, and which is still furnished in a Revolutionary style. (269 Monument Street, ☎ (978) 369-3909. www.thetrustees.org ① Mid-Apr-Oct: Mon-Sat: 10am-5pm. Sun: 12noon-5pm. Admission charge. *2 admissions for the price of 1 with voucher on page 71*.)

You can see another house inhabited by Hawthorne, **The Wayside** (455 Lexington Road, ☎ (978) 369-6975, ① Mid-May-Oct: Thu-Tue: 10am-5pm, Wed: closed, Nov-Mid-May: closed, admission charge), where he lived until his death in 1864.

The house had briefly belonged to the Alcott family, though they later moved to **Orchard House** where they stayed for 20 years. It was at Orchard House that Louisa May Alcott wrote her famous novel *Little Women*, and many of the original furnishings remain. (399 Lexington Road, ☎ (978) 369-4118. www.louisamayalcott.org ① Apr-Oct: Mon-Sat: 10am-4.30pm. Sun: 1pm-4.30pm. Nov-Mar: Mon-Fri: 11am-3pm. Sat: 10am-4.30pm. Sun: 1pm-4.30pm. Jan 1-15, Christmas, Easter & Thanksgiving: closed. Admission charge. *2 admissions for the price of 1 with voucher on page 71*.)

Having recently celebrated its 200th anniversary, the **Peabody Essex Museum** has long been an important part of New England's legacy to art and culture. The museum's vast collection includes exhibits on Native American, Asian and African art and culture, maritime art, decorative arts, architecture and photography. (East India Square, Salem, ☎ (978) 745-9500/(800) 745-4054. www.pem.org ① Apr-Oct: Mon-Sat: 10am-5pm. Sun: 12noon-5pm. Nov-Mar: Tue-Sat: 10am-5pm. Sun: 12noon-5pm. Mon: closed. Admission charge. *2 admissions for the price of 1 with voucher on page 71*.)

Reflections

"What a glorious morning this is" – Revolutionary leader Samuel Adams on hearing guns at Lexington, April 19, 1775

Dining

Boston has made great strides from the staunch dining traditions of its old New England roots. Not surprisingly, seafood is omnipresent, and chowder holds a special place in the hearts of Bostonians. **Legal Sea Foods** (800 Boylston Street, with other locations, ☎ 266-6800), **Turner Fisheries** (Westin Hotel, 10 Huntington Avenue, Ⓜ Back Bay/Copley, ☎ 424-7425), and **East Coast Grill & Raw Bar** are considered the best.

East Coast Grill & Raw Bar

1271 Cambridge Street, Cambridge
Ⓜ Central
☎ 491-6568

A specialty here is the brewpub, and good burger joints are plentiful. Some of the best are **Tim's Tavern** (329 Columbus Ave, Ⓜ Back Bay, ☎ 437-6898), the stylish **Audubon Circle** and **Mr. & Mrs. Bartley's** (1246 Massachusetts Avenue, Ⓜ Harvard, ☎ 354-6559) of Harvard Square.

Audubon Circle

838 Beacon Street
Ⓜ Kenmore Square
☎ 421-1910

The Pan-Asian trend continues to dominate the wave of cutting-edge cuisine and is exemplified by restaurants such as **P.F. Chang's** (8 Park Plaza, Ⓜ Boylston, ☎ 573-0821), **Pho Republique** (1415 Washington Street, Ⓜ Back Bay, ☎ 262-0005) and Wellesley's **Blue Ginger** (583 Washington Street, Wellesley, ☎ (781) 283-5790).

The Mediterranean trend has led to an influx of tapas-style places like **Sophia's** (1270 Boylston Street, Ⓜ Kenmore, ☎ 351-7001), **Dali** (415 Washington Street, Ⓜ Harvard, ☎ 661-3254) and **Tapeo** (266 Newbury Street, Ⓜ Copley, ☎ 267-4799). This new style has also become the trademark of several local chefs, including Todd English of **Olives**, which has been so popular that branches have been opened as far away as Las Vegas.

Outdoor dining on Newbury Street

Ranked the top restaurant in all of Boston, **Aujourd'hui** serves new American cuisine from a posh setting in the Four Seasons Hotel in Beacon Hill.

High atop the Prudential Center, **Top of the Hub** (800 Boylston Street, Ⓜ Prudential, ☎ 536-1775) is slowly earning the reputation for its food that it has long held for its unbeatable views. The **Bay Tower** *(60 State Street,* **M** *State Street/Government Center,* ☎ *723-1666)* is another fine room with a view. Located on the 33rd floor of Faneuil Hall Marketplace, it's a top spot for special occasions.

French cuisine still rules the list of Boston's top fine-dining establishments, however. **L'Espalier** continually tops that list. Other Gallic pleasers are **Aquitaine** *(569 Tremont,* **M** *Back Bay,* ☎ *424-8577)* and **Truc** *(560 Tremont,* **M** *Back Bay,* ☎ *338-8070).*

The **North End** is Boston's Little Italy. The neighborhood is awash with restaurants, specialty shops and cafés. For traditional dining, you might try **Pagliuca's** *(14 Parmenter Street,* **M** *Haymarket,* ☎ *367-1504)* or **Pomodoro** *(319 Hanover Street,* **M** *Haymarket,* ☎ *367-4348).* For something a little more creative and unusual, try **Marcuccio's** *(125 Salem Street,* **M** *Haymarket,* ☎ *723-1807)* or **Sage** *(69 Prince Street,* **M** *Haymarket,* ☎ *248-8814).* If seafood Italian-style is what you're after, don't miss **Daily Catch** *(323 Hanover Street and other branches,* **M** *Haymarket,* ☎ *523-8567).* The menu is built upon Sicilian family recipes.

For a cheap, fun dining experience, head to Boston's **Chinatown** (page 17). Strict vegetarians will appreciate **Buddha's Delight** *(3 Beach Street,* **M** *Coolidge Corner,* ☎ *739-8830),* while seafood-lovers will eat up the delectable chow at basement dive **Ho Yuen Ting Seafood** *(13A Hudson Street,* **M** *Chinatown,* ☎ *426-2316).* Another favorite that puts food over atmosphere is **Chau Chow City** *(52 Beach Street,* **M** *Coolidge Corner,* ☎ *426-6266).* For huge bowls of noodles at rock-bottom prices, visit Vietnamese **Pho Pasteur** *(682 Washington Street,* **M** *Chinatown,* ☎ *482-7467),* which has other locations throughout Boston. **Ginza** is known as the best Japanese restaurant.

Historical restaurants and taverns are plentiful in and around Boston. For a taste of the Old World, visit **Barker Tavern** *(21 Barker Road, Scituate,* ☎ *(781) 545-6533),* set in a 1634 house in Scituate, Concord's 1760 **Colonial Inn** *(48 Monument Square, Concord,* ☎ *(978) 369-9200)* or the 1826 **Union Oyster House** (page 11).

Olives

10 City Square, Charlestown
M Bunker Hill
☎ 242-1999

Aujourd'hui

200 Boylston Street
M Arlington/Boylston
☎ 351-2071

L'Espalier

30 Gloucester Street
M Hynes Convention Center/ICA
☎ 262-3023

Ginza

16 Hudson Street
M Chinatown
☎ 338-2261

Shopping

Shopping in Boston runs the gamut from the affordable to the outrageous, but across the board, shoppers are most delighted with the favorable sales tax laws. In the state of Massachusetts there is no sales tax on food purchases (except in restaurants), or on clothing below $175. Anything above that amount is subject to a 5% tax, well below that of most states.

Indoor shopping malls are plentiful in Boston as are abundant outlets of national chains. Typical of the 21st-century American city, there seems to be a Starbucks and a Gap on every corner.

The most famous shopping destination in Boston is undoubtedly historic **Faneuil Hall** and the adjacent **Quincy Market**. Built early in the 19th century, the warehouses of this former marketplace have been restored and are now chock full of vendors selling everything from traditional arts and crafts to the latest fashions. On Fridays and Saturdays, you can browse the open-air **Haymarket** where a variety of fresh goods are sold.

Downtown Crossing is a traffic-free pedestrian mall complete with street performers, food carts and outdoor kiosks. This is where to find **Filene's** department store and its discount emporium **Filene's Basement**. Urban legends have evolved from the tales of fist fights and other shenanigans sparked by this original bargain basement's major sales.

On and around **Boylston Street**, more than one hundred stores can be found, including the posh **Prudential Center** shopping mall, anchored by **Saks Fifth Avenue** and **Lord & Taylor**, and **Copley Place**, an even more exclusive shopping center anchored by **Neiman Marcus** and bursting with luxury goods retailers such as Tiffany & Co. and Gucci.

Following Boylston Street to its eastern end, at **Arlington Street**, you will find the **Heritage on the Garden** complex of condominiums and designer boutiques including **Hermès** *(22 Arlington Street,* *Arlington,* ☎ *482-8707),* **Escada** *(308 Boylston Street,* *Arlington,* ☎ *437-1200)* and

Filene's

426 Washington Street
Ⓜ Downtown Crossing
☎ 357-2100

Prudential Center

800 Boylston Street
Ⓜ Prudential

Copley Place

100 Avenue of the Arts
Ⓜ Copley

Shreve, Crump and Low

330 Boylston Street
Ⓜ Arlington
☎ 267-9100

Sonia Rykiel *(280 Boylston Street, Ⓜ Arlington, ☎ 426-2033)*. Across the street, you will find the legendary Boston institution **Shreve, Crump and Low**. In business since 1796, it is perhaps best known for its jewelry department.

If you're looking for unique items, head for **Charles Street** or **River Street**, in Beacon Hill, one of the best-known places for antique shopping in town. The **Boston Antique Co-op** offers two floors of antiques and collectables, while the **Cambridge Antique Market** *(201 Monsignor O'Brien Highway, Ⓜ Lechmere, ☎ 868-9655)* is a conglomerate of over 150 individual dealers.

Shopping in the Back Bay

Lined with Victorian buildings, **Newbury Street** is one of the city's prettiest shopping streets. It offers everything from chi-chi boutiques to chain record stores like **Tower Records**. The **Society of Arts and Crafts** *(175 Newbury Street, Ⓜ Copley, ☎ 266-1810)* is worth a look. The oldest non-profit craft organization in the U.S., it offers fine American craft works.

For those with a rich man's taste on a poor man's budget, there are several second-hand stores on Newbury that offer gently worn fine clothing. Women will want to visit **Chic Repeats** *(117 Newbury Street, Ⓜ Copley, ☎ 536-8580)*, while **The Closet** has both women's and men's clothing *(175 Newbury Street, Ⓜ Copley, ☎ 536-1919)*.

Harvard and **Central Squares**, in **Cambridge**, provide plenty of affordable shopping opportunities. The streets surrounding Harvard University are filled with budget shops catering to the student population. There are late-opening record stores, countless bookshops and some of the best vintage clothing shops in town. Don't miss the funky **Allston** neighborhood, just across the Charles River and centered on **Harvard Avenue**.

Boston Antique Co-op

119 Charles Street
Ⓜ Charles
☎ 227-9810

Tower Records

360 Newbury Street
Ⓜ Hynes Convention Center/ICA
☎ 247-5900

Nightlife and Performing Arts

From world-class performing arts organizations to some of the best Irish pubs in the U.S., Boston nightlife offers something for everyone.

The bar scene is diverse enough to please cap-wearing college students, black-clad hipsters and besuited sophisticates alike. "Blue laws" remain from more puritanical times, closing down the bars at 2am. The drinking age is 21 and bars adhere to this strictly; be prepared to show identification.

Undoubtedly the most famous bar is Boston is the **Bull & Finch Pub**, better known as the inspiration for *Cheers*. Literally brought over piece by piece from England, this pub is packed with tourists nightly. If you must see it, opt instead for a drink upstairs at the **Library Grill at the Hampshire House** (Ⓜ *Arlington*, ☎ *227-9600*), where a pianist, oil paintings and dark paneling create a refined atmosphere.

For something more casual, check out the **Sunset Grill & Tap** in Allston where you will find hundreds of beers to choose from *(130 Brighton Avenue, ☎ 254-1331)*. Across the river in Cambridge, you can visit the **Cambridge Brewing Company** *(1 Kendall Square, Building 100, Ⓜ Kendall/MIT, ☎ 494-1994)* and **John Harvard's Brew House** in Harvard Square.

The theater scene in Boston is going strong and many Broadway-bound shows do a run here before hitting the Great White Way. **Bostix** *(Faneuil Hall, with additional branches in Copley Square and Harvard Square)* is the main source of information for concerts and the theater, as well as a ticketing agency. It is best known for the half-price, day of performance tickets it sells from 11am. Bring cash or travelers' checks and choose from the shows posted at the booth.

Classical aficionados are probably familiar with the fine reputation of the **Boston Symphony** (☎ *542-6772*), founded in 1881, **Boston Philharmonic** (☎ *496-2222*) and the forever-televised **Boston Pops** (☎ *266-1492*). There are also countless church and university concerts and a host of chamber music, choral and early music groups. For opera, the **Boston Lyric Opera** is the town's

Bull & Finch Pub

84 Beacon Street
Ⓜ Arlington/Charles
☎ 227-9605

John Harvard's Brew House

33 Dunster Street
Ⓜ Harvard
☎ 868-3585

Bostix

Faneuil Hall
Ⓜ Government Center,
State Street or
Haymarket
☎ 723-5181

Shubert Theater

265 Tremont Street
Ⓜ Boylston/Chinatown
☎ 482-9393

sole professional company *(114 State Street,* Ⓜ *State Street,* ☎ *542-6772).*

The main classical dance organization is the **Boston Ballet** *(☎ 695-6950)* which performs at both the **Shubert Theater** and the 3,700-seat **Wang Center for the Performing Arts**. The **Ballet Theater of Boston** focuses on original works and reinventing the classics *(186 Massachusetts Ave.,* Ⓜ *Massachusetts Ave,* ☎ *262-0961).* For contemporary dance, the **Dance Collective** *(☎ 492-0444)* stages shows at various venues.

If it's jazz you're after, **Scullers Jazz Club** *(400 Soldiers Field Road,* Ⓜ *Central,* ☎ *783-0811)* in the Doubletree Guest Suites in Allston recruits some big-name performers, as does **Regattabar** *(1 Bennett Street,* Ⓜ *Harvard,* ☎ *864-1200)* in the Charles Hotel in Harvard Square. For local musicians, try **Wally's** *(427 Massachusetts Ave,* Ⓜ *Massachusetts Ave,* ☎ *424-1408).*

For live music, the **Middle East** *(472 Massachusetts Avenue,* Ⓜ *Central,* ☎ *497-0576)* and **Paradise Rock Club** *(967 Commonwealth Avenue,* Ⓜ *Pleasant Street,* ☎ *562-8800)* host the best in local rock bands as well as smaller national acts.

If you are looking to dance the night away, Boston's biggest club is the **Roxy**, set in a renovated ballroom. It hosts a variety of theme nights covering everything from swing to Latin to Jamaican. Theme nights at another big club, **Axis** *(13 Lansdowne Street,* Ⓜ *Kenmore Square,* ☎ *262-2437),* include techno, gay and live music night.

Wang Center for the Performing Arts

270 Tremont Street
Ⓜ Boylston/Chinatown
☎ 482-9393

Roxy

279 Tremont Street
Ⓜ Boylston/Chinatown
☎ 338-7699

Downtown Boston illuminated at night

Visitor Information

Harvard in the spring

CLIMATE

New England summers can be humid and hot, and winters can be harsh. Spring and fall are undoubtedly the best time to visit, though the city can be incredibly charming during a thick winter snowfall.

CHILDREN

Boston is a history lesson brought to life, but in no way does it have to be boring to be educational. Kids of all ages will enjoy the wealth of sights and attractions of America's "cradle of liberty". They'll enjoy throwing chests of tea overboard at the **Boston Tea Party Ship and Museum** (page 16) as well as connecting other historic events to attractions along the **Freedom Trail** (page 18).

Other spots of special interest to children include the **New England Aquarium** (page 15), the **Charles Hayden Planetarium** (23), the **Museum of Transportation** (page 45), the **Harvard Museum of Natural History** (page 40), the **Peabody Museum** (page 41), the **Sports Museum of New England** (page 22), the **John Hancock Observatory** (page 32) and, of course, the **Children's Museum of Boston** (page 16).

The **Greater Boston Convention & Visitors' Bureau** (page 60) publishes a free, comprehensive guide called *Kids Love Boston* which is highly recommended for its kid's-eye view.

HEALTH AND SAFETY

Doctors – In the Yellow Pages, look under "Physicians and Surgeons" to find doctors.

Drugstores / Pharmacies (open 24 hours) –
In the Yellow Pages, look under
"Pharmacies" for a comprehensive list.
Many pharmacies are open 24 hours,
including the CVS chain (*155-157 Charles
Street, ☎ 523-1028, additional locations
throughout Boston*).

Hospitals (with 24-hour emergency rooms)
– Massachusetts General Hospital (*55 Fruit
Street, ☎ 726-2000*); Beth Israel Deaconess
Medical Center (*330 Brookline Avenue,
☎ 667-7000*); New England Medical Center
(*750 Washington Street, ☎ 636-5000*).

You will be required to pay for any medical
treatment you receive, so it is advisable to
take out comprehensive travel and health
insurance before arriving.

Safety – Boston is generally quite safe,
though caution should be exercised
outside the most visited parts of town.
Wandering off the beaten path is not
advisable unless you know where you are
going. As in any other large city, you
should protect your valuables and watch
out for pickpockets in crowded areas,
particularly in and around the busier
tourist sites such as Quincy Market.

HOTELS

The relative scarcity of hotel rooms in
Boston means that availability is often
tight. Rates overall are quite expensive
and can soar on weekends and at holiday
times, so it is always advisable to book as
far ahead as possible. 💰 = under $100
per double room per night, 💰 💰 = $100-
150, 💰 💰 💰 = $150-200, 💰 💰 💰 💰 =
$200 and upwards.

Back Bay

Chandler Inn (*26 Chandler Street, ☎ 482-
3450.*) 💰 - 💰 💰

Midtown Hotel (*220 Huntington Avenue
(Avenue of the Arts), ☎ 262-1000 or (800) 343-
1177.*) 💰 💰 - 💰 💰 💰

Marriott Hotel at Copley Place (*110
Huntington Avenue (Avenue of the Arts), ☎
236-5800 or (800) 228-9290.*) 💰 💰 💰 -
💰 💰 💰 💰

Ritz-Carlton (*15 Arlington Street, ☎ 536-5700
or (800) 241-3333.*) 💰 💰 💰 💰

CUSTOMS

All visitors to the U.S.
must have a valid
passport, a visitor's visa
and a valid onward
passage ticket.
Passport holders from
the UK, Canada, New
Zealand, Japan and all
western European
countries (with the
exception of Ireland,
Portugal, Greece and
Vatican City) are not
required to have a visa
if staying for fewer than
90 days.

ELECTRIC CURRENT

The U.S. uses 110V (60
hz) and most appliances
from overseas will
require a transformer.
Check with your hotel
regarding sockets for
electrical devices.

EMERGENCIES

Dial ☎ 911 for the
police, the fire service
or an ambulance.

Four Seasons *(200 Boylston Street, ☎ 338-4400 or (800) 332-3442.)* 💰 💰 💰 💰

Eliot Hotel *(370 Commonwealth Avenue, ☎ 267-1607 or (800) 443-5468.)* 💰 💰 💰 💰

Beacon Hill

John Jeffries House *(14 Embankment Road, ☎ 367-1866.)* 💰 - 💰 💰

Beacon Hill Bed and Breakfast *(27 Brimmer Street, ☎ 523-7376.)* 💰 💰 - 💰 💰 💰

Downtown

Le Meridien Hotel *(250 Franklin Street, ☎ 451-1900 or (800) 543-4300.)* 💰 💰 💰 💰

Omni Parker House *(60 School Street, ☎ 227-8600 or (800) 843-6664.)* 💰 💰 💰 - 💰 💰 💰 💰

Harborside Inn *(185 State Street, ☎ 723-7500.)* 💰 💰 - 💰 💰 💰

Seaport Hotel *(1 Seaport Lane, ☎ 385-4000 or (877) 732-7678.)* 💰 💰 💰 - 💰 💰 💰 💰

Cambridge

Doubletree Guest Suites *(400 Soldiers Field Road, ☎ 783-0090 or (800) 222-8733.)* 💰 💰

Inn at Harvard *(1201 Massachusetts Avenue, ☎ 491-2222 or (800) 458-5886.)* 💰 💰 💰 - 💰 💰 💰 💰

The Charles Hotel *(1 Bennett Street, ☎ 864-1200 or (800) 882-1818.)* 💰 💰 💰 💰

OPENING HOURS

Banks – Generally, banks are open Mon-Fri: 9.30am-3pm or 3.30pm. Some branches are open later and some are also open on Saturday mornings. ATMs can be found just about anywhere, including in most of the casinos.

Bars / restaurants – The law prohibits bars from opening past 2am and this rule is strictly followed.

Shops – Stores are generally open between 9-10am and 6-7pm (later on Thursdays), and many malls and major department stores are open until 9pm. In touristy areas and around the universities, even independent shops tend to remain open late most days.

RESTROOMS/TOILETS

There is the occasional restroom in Boston, but more likely, you will have to seek one out in a restaurant, bar or hotel.

SPECIAL TRAVELERS

Disabled – Most of Boston's hotels, attractions and restaurants have facilities for the disabled. It is nonetheless advised to call ahead and get details. The **Massachusetts Office on Disability** (☎ 727-7440, (800) 642-0249) can provide travelers with information about visiting Boston.

Senior citizens – Seniors (generally defined as 65 or older) usually receive reduced admission at attractions. This is in addition to the *for less* discounts they can obtain with this guide.

Students – The International Student Identity Card is necessary for students to obtain concessions. It can be purchased from the **Council on International Educational Exchange** (☎ (888) 268-6245).

Gay and lesbian – There is an active gay scene in Boston, centering predominantly in the South End. Local resources include the **Gay and Lesbian Helpline** (☎ 267-9001).

TELEPHONES

When dialing within Boston you do not need to dial the 617 area code, but only the seven-digit telephone number.

MONEY

Currency - The American currency is the dollar ($), consisting of 100 cents (¢). There are four commonly used American coins: penny (1 cent), nickel (5 cents), dime (10 cents), quarter (25 cents). Notes, which are also known as bills, come in $1, $2, $5, $10, $20, $50 and $100 denominations.

Money changing - You can change money at banks or at bureaux de change. Although bureaux de change stay open longer, they sometimes charge high commissions (transaction fees).

Credit cards - Major credit cards are accepted just about everywhere.

Newbury Street

Any phone number in this book listed with an area code means that it is outside the 617 dialing area, and you must dial 1+area code+phone number (e.g. 1-800-555-1234). A call within Boston costs 35 cents from a public phone.

TIPPING

Tipping is customary in Boston, even for the most basic services. Although tipping may seem strange to some overseas visitors, keep in mind that a service charge is rarely included and that employers are not required by law to pay tipped employees the minimum wage.

Restaurants – A 15-20% tip on the total bill is standard.

Taxis / bartenders / hairdressers – The standard tip is 15-20%.

Porters / bellhops – The normal tip is $1 per bag, depending on the number of bags and the distance carried.

Coat check – Generally tip $1 per piece.

Hotel maids – The normal tip is $1 per day.

TOURS

Bus – **Brush Hill Gray Line Tours** (435 High Street, Randolph, ☎ (781) 986-6100) offers full and half day tours of Boston and the surrounding areas. Tours include complimentary pick-up and return from many greater Boston hotels.

Boat – **Boston Harbor Cruises** (1 Long Wharf, ☎ 227-4321) and **Odyssey Cruises** (Atlantic Avenue at Rowes Wharf, 654-9700) offer various boat tours of Boston Harbor. You can also sail the harbor on **Boston's Tall Ships** (67 Long Wharf, ☎ 742-0333), the schooners Liberty and Liberty Clipper.

Amphibious – For a truly unique experience, take **Boston Duck Tours** (790 Boylston Street, ☎ 723-3825) through the streets of Boston and into the Charles River on a genuine Second World War amphibious vehicle.

Walking – The Freedom Trail (page 18) is one of the most famous walking tours in the country, with good reason – it covers

TAXES

The U.S. does not have an export tax program or a value added tax (VAT). Instead, all shoppers are required to pay state sales tax (currently 5% in Massachusetts) when purchasing goods valued at over $175 (see *Shopping* (pages 52-53) for more information).

TOURIST INFORMATION

The **Greater Boston Convention & Visitors' Bureau** (☎ 536-4100) is a valuable source for information and operates visitor information kiosks throughout the city.

TRAVELING FROM THE AIRPORT

Logan International Airport (☎ (800) 235-6426) is located just across the harbor from downtown Boston.

almost all of the major historic sites in Boston. There is also a **Black Heritage Trail** (page 21), **Irish Immigrant Trail** and several others covering different themes. Trail maps and information can be found at the **Greater Boston Convention & Visitors' Bureau** (page 60) or information kiosks located throughout Boston.

A "T"sign

TRAVELING IN BOSTON

Buses – Public buses run from approximately 5.30am to 12.30pm. Contact the **Massachusetts Bay Transportation Authority** (MBTA) for information on routes and schedules (☎ 222-3200).

Car – Traveling by car is not recommended as parking is difficult and public transportation is quite efficient. A car can be useful, however, for out-of-town trips. Some of the biggest agencies are **Avis** (☎ (800) 331-1212), **Hertz** (☎ (800) 654-3131) and **Budget** (☎ (800) 527-0700).

Taxis – Cabs are available throughout Boston and at the airport. There is an initial fare, then an additional fee for mileage. You can also phone cab companies direct. Try **Checker** (☎ 536-7000) or **Town Taxi** (☎ 536-5000).

"T" – "T" is the abbreviation used to designate Boston's public transportation system – the **Massachusetts Bay Transportation Authority** – of trains, subways and trolleys. The four lines, red, green, blue and orange, intersect in downtown Boston. As well as single journey tickets, there are visitor passes which are valid for one, three or seven days of unlimited travel. The system runs from 5.30am until half past midnight every day. For more information call the MBTA on ☎ 222-3200 or ☎ (800) 392-6100.

CREDITS

Text: Christina Prostano

Principal Photography: Cambridge Tourism, Massachusetts Tourism, Society for the Preservation of New England Antiquities, JFK Library, The Children's Museum, MIT Museum, Museum of Fine Arts, Museum of Transportation, New England Aquarium, The Paul Revere Memorial Association.

Index

New England Aquarium

2 admissions for the price of 1 at the
New England Aquarium (page 15)

Valid from March 1, 2000

Unforgettable Boston

2 admissions for the price of 1 at
Unforgettable Boston (page 16)

Valid from March 1, 2000

Boston Tea Party Ship & Museum

2 admissions for the price of 1 at the
Boston Tea Party Ship and Museum
(page16)

Valid from March 1, 2000

Children's Museum of Boston

2 admissions for the price of 1 at the
Children's Museum of Boston
(page 16)

Valid from March 1, 2000

Prescott House

2 admissions for the price of 1 at
Prescott House (page 19)

Valid from March 1, 2000

Nichols House Museum

2 admissions for the price of 1 at the
Nichols House Museum (page 20)

Valid from March 1, 2000

Harrison Gray Otis House

2 admissions for the price of 1 at the
Harrison Gray Otis House (page 21)

Valid from March 1, 2000

This voucher entitles the holder to the following discount at the **New England Aquarium** (page 15):

2-for-1 admission: one free admission with each admission of equal or greater value purchased

This voucher entitles the holder to the following discount at **Unforgettable Boston** (page 16):

2-for-1 admission: one free admission with each admission of equal or greater value purchased

This voucher entitles the holder to the following discount at the **Boston Tea Party Ship and Museum** (page 16):

2-for-1 admission: one free admission with each admission of equal or greater value purchased

This voucher entitles the holder to the following discount at the **Children's Museum of Boston** (p.16):

2-for-1 admission: one free admission with each admission of equal or greater value purchased

This voucher entitles the holder to the following discount at **Prescott House** (page 19):

2-for-1 admission: one free admission with each admission of equal or greater value purchased

This voucher entitles the holder to the following discount at the **Nichols House Museum** (page 20):

2-for-1 admission: one free admission with each admission of equal or greater value purchased

This voucher entitles the holder to the following discount at the **Harrison Gray Otis House** (page 21):

2-for-1 admission: one free admission with each admission of equal or greater value purchased

Sports Museum

2 admissions fo[r]
the **Sports Museu**[m]
(pa[ge])

Valid from March 1, 2000

Charles Hayden Planetarium

2 admissions for the price of 1 at the
Charles Hayden Planetarium (page 23)

Valid from March 1, 2000

Paul Revere House

2 admissions for the price of 1 at the
Paul Revere House (page 24)

Valid from March 1, 2000

Gibson House Museum

2 admissions for the price of 1 at the
Gibson House Museum (page 30)

Valid from March 1, 2000

John Hancock Tower Observatory

2 admissions for the price of 1 at the
John Hancock Tower Observatory (p. 32)

Valid from March 1, 2000. Discount not
applicable on July 4th.

Institute of Contemporary Art

2 admissions for the price of 1 at the
Institute of Contemporary Art (page 34)

Valid from March 1, 2000

Museum of Fine Arts

$2 off admission to the **Museum of
Fine Arts** (page 35)

Voucher valid for up to two people.

Please circle as appropriate: **1   2**

Valid from March 1, 2000

This voucher entitles the holder to the following discount at the **Sports Museum** (page 22):

2-for-1 admission: one free admission with each admission of equal or greater value purchased

This voucher entitles the holder to the following discount at the **Charles Hayden Planetarium** (page 23):

2-for-1 admission: one free admission with each admission of equal or greater value purchased

This voucher entitles the holder to the following discount at the **Paul Revere House** (page 24):

2-for-1 admission: one free admission with each admission of equal or greater value purchased

This voucher entitles the holder to the following discount at the **Gibson House Museum** (p. 30):

2-for-1 admission: one free admission with each admission of equal or greater value purchased

This voucher entitles the holder to the following discount at the **John Hancock Tower Observatory** (p.32):

2-for-1 admission: one free admission with each admission of equal or greater value purchased

This voucher entitles the holder to the following discount at the **Institute of Contemporary Art** (page 34):

2-for-1 admission: one free admission with each admission of equal or greater value purchased

This voucher entitles the holder to the following discount at the **Museum of Fine Arts** (page 35):

$2 off admission

Photographic Resource Center

2 admissions for the price of 1 at the **Photographic Resource Center** (page 36)

Valid from March 1, 2000

Harvard Museum of Natural History

2 admissions for the price of 1 at the **Harvard Museum of Natural History** (page 40)

Valid from March 1, 2000

Peabody Museum of Archaeology and Ethnology

2 admissions for the price of 1 at the **Peabody Museum of Archaeology and Ethnology** (page 41)

Valid from March 1, 2000

MIT Museum

2 admissions for the price of 1 at the **MIT Museum** (page 44)

Valid from March 1, 2000

Museum of Transportation

2 admissions for the price of 1 at the **Museum of Transportation** (page 45)

Valid from March 1, 2000

Shirley-Eustis House

2 admissions for the price of 1 at the **Shirley-Eustis House** (page 46)

Valid from March 1, 2000

Museum of the National Center of Afro-American Artists

2 admissions for the price of 1 at the **Museum of the National Center of Afro-American Artists** (page 46)

Valid from March 1, 2000

This voucher entitles the holder to the following discount at the **Photographic Resource Center** (page 36):

2-for-1 admission: one free admission with each admission of equal or greater value purchased

This voucher entitles the holder to the following discount at the **Harvard Museum of Natural History** (page 40):

2-for-1 admission: one free admission with each admission of equal or greater value purchased

This voucher entitles the holder to the following discount at the the **Peabody Museum of Archaeology and Ethnology** (page 41):

2-for-1 admission: one free admission with each admission of equal or greater value purchased

This voucher entitles the holder to the following discount at the **MIT Museum** (page 44):

2-for-1 admission: one free admission with each admission of equal or greater value purchased

This voucher entitles the holder to the following discount at the **Museum of Transportation** (p. 45):

2-for-1 admission: one free admission with each admission of equal or greater value purchased

This voucher entitles the holder to the following discount at the **Shirley-Eustis House** (page 46):

2-for-1 admission: one free admission with each admission of equal or greater value purchased

This voucher entitles the holder to the following discount at the **Museum of the National Center of Afro-American Artists** (page 46):

2-for-1 admission: one free admission with each admission of equal or greater value purchased

JFK Library and Museum

2 admissions for the price of 1 at the
JFK Library and Museum (page 46)

Valid from March 1, 2000

Josiah Quincy House

2 admissions for the price of 1 at
Josiah Quincy House (page 47)

Valid from March 1, 2000

Codman House

2 admissions for the price of 1 at
Codman House (page 48)

Valid from March 1, 2000

Gropius House

2 admissions for the price of 1 at
Gropius House (page 48)

Valid from March 1, 2000

Buckman Tavern

2 admissions for the price of 1 at
Buckman Tavern (page 48)

Valid from March 1, 2000

Hancock-Clarke House

2 admissions for the price of 1 at the
Hancock-Clarke House (page 48)

Valid from March 1, 2000

Munroe Tavern

2 admissions for the price of 1 at
Munroe Tavern (page 48)

Valid from March 1, 2000

This voucher entitles the holder
to the following discount at the
JFK Library and Museum (p. 46):

2-for-1 admission: one free
admission with each admission of
equal or greater value purchased

This voucher entitles the holder
to the following discount at
Josiah Quincy House (page 47):

2-for-1 admission: one free
admission with each admission of
equal or greater value purchased

This voucher entitles the holder
to the following discount at
Codman House (page 48):

2-for-1 admission: one free
admission with each admission of
equal or greater value purchased

This voucher entitles the holder
to the following discount at
Gropius House (page 48):

2-for-1 admission: one free
admission with each admission of
equal or greater value purchased

This voucher entitles the holder
to the following discount at
Buckman Tavern (page 48):

2-for-1 admission: one free
admission with each admission of
equal or greater value purchased

This voucher entitles the holder
to the following discount at the
Hancock-Clarke House (p. 48):

2-for-1 admission: one free
admission with each admission of
equal or greater value purchased

This voucher entitles the holder
to the following discount at
Munroe Tavern (page 48):

2-for-1 admission: one free
admission with each admission of
equal or greater value purchased

Old Manse

2 admissions for the price of 1 at
Old Manse (page 49)

Valid from March 1, 2000

Orchard House

2 admissions for the price of 1 at
Orchard House (page 49)

Valid from March 1, 2000

Peabody Essex Museum

2 admissions for the price of 1 at the
Peabody Essex Museum (page 49)

Valid from March 1, 2000

Customer Response Card

We would like to hear your comments about the
Boston for less Compact Guide so that we can improve it.
Please complete the information below and mail this card.
One card will be picked out at random to win a free holiday.
No stamp is required, either in the U.S. or your own country.

Name: ....

Address: ....

....

Tel. no.: ....

If you bought the book, where did you buy it from?.............

....

If you were given the book, which tour operator gave it
to you? ....

Number of people travelling in your party ....

How many days were you in Boston? ....

Did you like the guidebook?...

What did you like about it?..

....

Would you recommend it to a friend?...

Would you be more interested in a tour operator's
package if you knew it included the ***Boston for less
Compact Guide?*** ....

Any other comments ....

....

....

This voucher entitles the holder to the following discount at **Old Manse** (page 49):

2-for-1 admission: one free admission with each admission of equal or greater value purchased

This voucher entitles the holder to the following discount at **Orchard House** (page 49):

2-for-1 admission: one free admission with each admission of equal or greater value purchased

This voucher entitles the holder to the following discount at the **Peobody Essex Museum** (p. 49):

2-for-1 admission: one free admission with each admission of equal or greater value purchased

NE PAS AFFRANCHIR

NO STAMP REQUIRED

By air mail
Par avion

IBRS/CCRI NUMBER: PHQ-D/2560/W

REPONSE PAYEE
GRANDE-BRETAGNE

Metropolis International (UK) Limited
222 Kensal Road
LONDON, GREAT BRITAIN
W10 5BN